Food4 Friends

OUTDOOR FUN

colophon

Editing Désirée Verkaar **Final editing** Fridie van Loon, Linda Mous **Styling** Lize Boer **Photography** Food4Eyes **Art direction** Sabine van Loon **Assistant publisher** Josje Kets **Publisher** Pieter Harts **English translation** Trahern Gemmell for Textcase, Hilversum, The Netherlands

© Visconti 2006

© English edition 2008
email info@miller-books.com
www.millerbooks.com

ISBN 978 90 8724 049 3

Your friends, the sun & delicious food

Dining 'al fresco' lends a feeling of freedom. The open sky immediately creates a relaxed, informal atmosphere, stimulating all the senses, while the fresh air whets your appetite for the meal ahead. And eating together signifies a certain cosiness, a pleasant sense of belonging – sharing, chatting, reminiscing about old times. There is simply no better way to spend time with your best friends than enjoying a delicious meal outdoors!

Maybe you have something to celebrate. A garden full of visitors, children at play, the coals in the barbecue grill glowing just right. What's the best way to really create a festive atmosphere? Or perhaps you and your friends are cooking in turns for each other, and you want to really outdo yourself this time, to create something truly special, even better than the last time: picking out wines, finding the perfect table decorations, deciding on a beautiful presentation for your food... Or maybe everybody just drops by one Sunday afternoon for a walk in the woods and a nice lunch in the garden – informal, everyone simply enjoying each other's company. But you still want to make the meal even more special. Whatever the occasion, this book will give you a heap of helpful tips and inspirational ideas to put together a truly unforgettable celebration – without the fuss. Because this is all about one thing in particular: planning it so that you can enjoy the festivities as much as your guests, without having to spend your party stressed out in the kitchen.

contents

Half the battle
(and the rest)

Relax. It's your friends who will be dropping by, not your in-laws or some official delegation! You don't have to get all flustered about perfectly adhering to any rules or proper etiquette; the important thing is that you are all together again, enjoying each other's company – and eating well. So consider the following tips as guidelines which will help everything go smoothly and give you the chance to make everyone feel at home. Naturally, these tips need not be followed to the letter, except rule number one: enjoy!

Planning

Decide well in advance which dishes you want to make, so that you can make your grocery lists, stock up on non-perishable items and place any orders you need. If you plan on cooking on a really large scale, it's always handy to plan out the order of events for the big day. Just write them up point by point, see what you are able to prepare a day or two beforehand and make an estimate of how much time you'll need for each dish, including plating and presentation. It's best not to get too optimistic here, otherwise the whole timetable might fall to pieces at the first obstacle. If you're someone who doesn't like standing in the kitchen for days on end, or simply don't have the time for it, then go for recipes which give you a pleasing result without too much work. You can simplify recipes or combine home-made dishes with well-chosen store-bought dishes. If you have a couple classy, impressive dishes, it's easy to bulk the meal up with simple sides: a fresh salad, a simple vegetable dish, or something from the deli. And test new recipes out first on your own before making them for others. This way, you are almost guaranteed success!

A beautiful, logical whole

It is not difficult to put a menu together, though there are a few things you need to take into consideration. The most important is variety. Two dishes with chicken, the same herb twice in a row or two fried dishes right after each other... That is going to get a little tiring. Pay special attention to the variety of ingredients and preparation methods. It is also a good idea to get a feel for a diversity of colours, textures (whether crunchy or soft) and composition. But... variety does not mean throwing a meal together out of the most contrary dishes and things which simply do not go together. Aim for a beautiful, logical whole. An Asian-oriented dessert, for instance, is going to fall out of step a bit if you're doing a Mediterranean menu. Of course, your cooking does not have to centre around a certain 'theme', but the important thing is that the style of all the dishes is harmonious.

Preparation is half the battle

The proper sequence of dishes is usually quite logical. Cold dishes should generally be served before warm ones, simple dishes before the more intricate ones, light before heavy and mild before spicy. For example: cold starter – soup – warm starter – main course; and fish – poultry – red meat – game. And, also important, pay attention to how much time each course will require, and what you can prepare in advance. If the main course is already laid out and just needs to be put in the oven, then you can opt for a more work-intensive starter.

Kitchen help

In some cases it is almost a matter of prestige that your guests get the feeling they're in a five-star restaurant. Usually, however, it doesn't have to be quite so formal, and in this case there are always people who don't mind helping out in the kitchen. It might be a good idea to leave something that needs peeling or slicing!. This way, if people do offer to help, you don't have to tell them there's nothing you can think of for them to do.

Otherwise, a simpler first course might be wise: a soup you can make the day before (it will only get better as it sits, trust me) or a salad. Especially when it comes to desserts, it's always nice to have things ready to set out, because there's a good chance that once you've finished the main course, with a full stomach and a couple glasses of wine behind you, you won't want to be racing back into the kitchen...

That special butcher's

The menu has been set and the itinerary all laid out – do you have enough time to get all your shopping done? Then go to a few good specialty shops. There's usually a particular one in the neighbourhood known for high quality: that special butcher, greengrocer or fishmonger (seller) who really has a feel for his products and a wonderfully vast knowledge of the subject. True, you often have to pay a little more. But the odds are good that you will be buying true quality, a good deal superior to anything you would find in a supermarket. And just as important: you get free advice along with it. Choose a moment when the shop is not too busy (in other words, not Saturday morning) and ask your cheese merchant, for instance, which cheeses will be perfectly ripe at the time and which wine he would recommend. Maybe you can try a piece or two to see what you like... Let your butcher know about the recipe you're planning, and you will likely end up with the perfect piece of meat for it. True experts are more than happy to spread some of their knowledge and enthusiasm about their products. If you require something special which is not in the shop, simply order it a week or so in advance.

Set the mood

If you're planning something really special, take some time beforehand to think about table decoration. Don't just worry about whether or not you have enough dishes and silverware (though this is important too of course), but most of all ask yourself: what kind of mood do I want to create at the table? With a little contemplation and a bit of work you can achieve breathtaking results. You don't have to worry about matching the dishes every time. If you have nice plates in a neutral colour, you can get a different effect each time just with the tablecloth, some decorations and careful lighting. The simpler presentations are actually the chic ones. One or two select eye-catchers do a lot more for a table setting than a whole bunch of little things together. You can always come up with a theme appropriate to the food being served. Orient this towards the current season, or a country or region (is it going to be a Mediterranean picnic? How about a Caribbean barbecue?). If you don't have any particular theme, then pick out a certain style: romantic, sleek and modern, rustic... Certain objects or materials go with different styles. Which associations do you make with, say, a rustic style? Take five or ten minutes to brainstorm and you will come up with plenty of ideas.

Tone on tone

You can also choose a colour or material as a motif. Select a particular base colour and work with all the various hues of that single colour. This will give you the 'tone on tone' effect, very atmospheric. This way the overall table setting will have a personal touch to it, because everything was chosen by yourself. All that attention to detail will immediately make your table look more inviting and hospitable, and might even make the food taste that much better.

A little attention

Of course, what goes for decorating the table also applies to the plates. You can even make a plateful of bangers and mash look like a culinary masterpiece if you just present it the right way! The opposite is true as well: the brilliant meal that you spent hours standing in the kitchen to prepare will not look like much if you serve it out of kitchen pots at a bare table. It only takes a little attention to such details to make a meal look and taste better. You can come up with all sorts of looks, but keep it simple. A very stark presentation can be extremely trendy, as evidenced in many Japanese restaurants. Three identically sized pieces of tuna arranged next to each other on a square plate, with matchstick-size pieces of cucumber and scallion. Or separate elements arranged in a square or triangle: a fish fillet, a mound of mixed greens, a stuffed mushroom. Whatever the presentation, remember to never fill the plate too full. There should be some space between the food and the edge of the plate, which should be wiped clean before serving.

Beds and towers

Consider replacing the traditional combination of meat, potatoes and veg on a single plate with a series of smaller dishes, for example a vegetable starter followed by the main course with a simple potato garnish. By spacing it out this way, you are also placing greater emphasis on the individual components of the meal. You can also set the table with separate serving bowls and let the guests help themselves. If you're serving something like rice or mashed potatoes, try using a steel cooking ring to get a nice, perfect circle. Cooking rings can also be used to shape the various components of the dish into a 'tower'. In any case, it's always a crowd-pleaser to add some height to the dishes being served. Meat should be sliced on the diagonal. Sauces can be drizzled around the dish for greatest effect. But not too much: extra sauce can always be set in a bowl on the table for whoever wants it.

Nice ingredients

Garnish with fresh ingredients, such as lettuce leaves (dressed) or anything else that goes with the dish. Think ahead and set some of the nicer ingredients aside to use for garnish. Even a little freshly ground pepper at the last minute can add a lot to a dish. Or drizzle a bit of olive oil around the food (if it's not out of place, add a few drops of balsamic vinegar as well; this will give the appearance of little 'eyes'). And a little fresh fruit and a dusting of confectioner's sugar can transform the most ordinary dessert. But remember: always opt for variety when it comes to the presentation. This means don't always resort to beds or towers...

It's the little things...

Some things are so right under your nose that you almost forget all about them.

- Read through all the recipes one more time on the day before. Have you neglected some beans that need soaking overnight, or meat that needs to marinade?
- Any drinks you plan on serving cold should be put in the fridge.
- Set the table before your guests arrive.
- Make sure they have a welcome drink and something to munch on.
- Tidy the kitchen up now and again as you cook to keep your work space clean and manageable.
- And remember: always taste the dishes before you serve them.
- For warm dishes, heat up the plates in the oven or microwave (wet them a bit first).
- Put dessert plates, ice cream dishes and cocktail glasses in the freezer.

About this book

Well, that covers the general tips. The following chapters contain plenty more specific tips – about decorating your garden as well as your table, about plating the food, and preparation, serving, combining, etc. You're free to combine the recipes as you wish, or follow one of the suggested menus at the end of each chapter. These menus even include wine advice and a complete step-by-step plan, so you won't overlook anything. All the recipes – unless otherwise noted – are written for four people. This is a handy number because it is so easy to calculate. Most recipes can simply be multiplied if needed, except for the amount of oil or butter listed for sautéing. This quantity should remain about the same.

picnic

Life's a picnic!

Whether lounging on the most nostalgic red-and-white chequered cloth with a wicker basket filled with home-made bread, cheeses, fresh fruit and cranberry muffins – or just pulling some hip finger-food out of the ice box - think crostini with chic peas and prawns. Or even doing the five-star thing, with champagne, a cool cucumber soup and smoked salmon quiches, the important thing is that you are all together, feeling the fresh grass between your toes and the spring sun on your faces.

Picnicking is all the rage again and has been for a couple years now. Even weddings are being celebrated on a blanket in the woods! This is a pleasantly informal way to do something special with a group of close friends, and a real change from the standard routine. Some people see the renaissance of this trend in Europe as arising from the influence of other cultures. For Turkish families for instance, it is a real tradition to go out into nature and enjoy a wide variety of home-made delicacies (which are often shared with casual passersby). Other people say that the trend comes more from the hectic pace of modern urban living, which makes us increasingly feel the need to (re)discover the great outdoors. Accompanied, of course, by such time-honoured products as artisanal cheeses and home-baked breads. It could just be that everything comes back into style after a while...

Relax!

However you do it, picnicking is a pleasant and playful way to surprise your friends. It goes without saying that this type of dining has a heap of advantages for the host or hostess, as it's really the least stressful way to receive guests. Just think about it: you don't have to spend all day cleaning the house and have no shortage of space for any number of guests. You don't have to worry about sitting around a table full of dirty dishes afterwards. And, above all: everything is ready and all packed up beforehand. There's no in-and-out of the kitchen, no fussing over the stove; you can kick back and relax along with your friends, prop yourself up against the trunk of a tree and just enjoy the good food and a little R & R. You can make the picnic basket as simple or intricate as you want, but arranging a nice picnic generally takes a lot less time (and money) than, say, a four-course meal at home. In this chapter you will find recipes for delicious sweet and savoury snacks to stock your ice box (chest), plus tips and ideas for planning a successful outing under the open sky. Whatever the occasion – from a birthday to 'just because' – it's picnic time!

Pique-nique chique

The word 'picnic' comes from the French 'pique-nique'. Originally, this simply meant 'a small meal'. Beginning in the eighteenth century, however, it referred to food eaten outside. Picnics at this time were often quite formal gatherings, not on a blanket in the grass, but around fancy tables full of porcelain and crystal. Another exciting idea! Pick out a spot in the forest, somewhere with a wooden table and benches. Bring along a nice table cloth and maybe some cushions to sit on, attractive dishes and nice glasses, cloth napkins and proper silverware. Arrange the picnic table as luxuriously as possible and get the decorations right from Mother Nature – you won't need to go far to find a colourful bouquet of wildflowers, or a branch full of pretty buds. Take along thermoses filled with iced water to fill an ice bucket for the champagne or white

Pique-nique chique

wine. Serve the food in separate courses: a cold soup, fancy salad, savoury pies and cold cuts or smoked fish (how about a whole smoked salmon!). And don't forget the camera!

Spanish Gazpacho

for 8 people
1 kg (2.2 lbs) tomatoes
2 cucumbers
1 sweet red pepper
1 onion, chopped
1 clove of garlic, peeled
1 Spanish red pepper, seeded
4 tbsp olive oil
2 tbsp sherry vinegar
flat-leaf parsley or coriander (cilantro)
salt and pepper
white bread

1 Peel and cut 1 ½ cucumber, ½ sweet pepper and the tomatoes into large pieces.

2 Puree these together with the onion, garlic and pepper in the blender and push the mixture through a sieve when done.

3 Season the soup with salt, pepper, olive oil and sherry vinegar to taste and keep in the freezer until very cold.

4 Cut the remaining vegetables into small cubes and serve in separate dishes with the soup, together with cubes of white bread.

5 To further chill the soup, you can add some crushed ice immediately before serving.

Tip: You can keep this soup ice-cold by keeping it in a thermos with a few ice cubes.

17

4-8 bagels
4-8 slices smoked salmon (lox)
1 shallot, finely chopped
100 ml white wine
250 g (9 oz) cream cheese
2 tbsp chives, finely chopped
salt and freshly ground pepper

Bagels with lox and cream cheese

1 Simmer the shallot with the wine and remove from the heat.
2 Mix with the cream cheese and the chives.
3 Season with salt and pepper to taste.
4 Serve the bagels with a slice of salmon topped with the cream cheese.

Crunchy chicken sandwich

200 g (7 oz) smoked chicken fillet - 0.5 dl whipping cream – 1 tbsp yoghurt – 1 sour apple – 2 tbsp chopped hazelnuts – 1 tsp chopped candied ginger – 12 slices sandwich bread – 8 slices fried bacon – 8 leaves iceberg lettuce

1 Chop the fillets into small pieces.
2 Combine the whipping cream and yoghurt and whisk until half-stiff.
3 Mix in the fillets.
4 Finely dice the apple and mix it into the whipped cream together with the hazelnuts.
5 Add ginger to taste.
6 Serve on sandwich bread with fried bacon and iceberg lettuce.

Prawn ciabattas

300 g (10.5 oz) Norwegian king
prawns
2 ciabattas
1 tsp curry powder
2 tbsp mango chutney
5 tbsp yoghurt
4 bak choy sprigs
salt and freshly ground pepper

1 Slice the ciabattas through the
   middle and hollow them out to
   within 1-2 cm (0.4" – 0.8") of the
   edge.
2 Mix the curry powder, prawns,
   chutney and yoghurt and season
   with salt and pepper to taste.
3 Cut the bak choy stems into
   strips and use the leaves for
   stuffing the ciabattas.
4 Continue stuffing the ciabattas
   with the prawn mixture and
   insert the bak choy stems.

Don't forget...

The hardest part of organising
a picnic is not forgetting
anything. Use this checklist or
make your own list of things
you want to bring along:

- Picnic blankets (one extra than
  you think you will need) and a
  plastic tarp to place underneath
- Plates, flatware, glasses, cups
- Serviettes
- Cutting board(s) and a
  good knife
- Serving spoons
- Corkscrew, tin opener,
  cheese slicer etc.
- Salt, pepper and sugar
- Moist towelettes
- Plastic bags for putting the
  rubbish and dirty plates in after
  the meal
- A first-aid kit with plasters,
  sunburn lotion and something
  for insect bites
- More than enough water to
  drink and maybe for washing
  as well
- Games or something to read
  Folding camping chairs or
  fisherman's stools if you want

Three-cheese ciabatta

4 Italian ciabattas – 1 aubergine, sliced – 6 tbsp olive oil – 4 tbsp ricotta – 50 g (1.75 oz) watercress – 50 g (1.75 oz) rocket – 50 g (1.75 oz) olives – 2 tbsp hazelnuts, roasted and chopped – 4 tomatoes, preferably oblong ones – 60 g (2 oz) gorgonzola, in pieces – 60 g (2 oz) Parmesan cheese, shaved

1 Fry the aubergine slices in the olive oil until golden brown.
2 Cut open the ciabattas and spread them with the ricotta. Top this with the watercress and rocket.
3 Stuff with the aubergine, tomato slices, olives and hazelnut pieces.
4 Lastly, add the slices of gorgonzola and Parmesan.

Fresh fruit

Deliciously juicy fruits should not be left out of any picnic basket. It's best to take them along whole (preferably in an ice box (chest)) and wait to clean them until you're at the picnic spot. This will keep them fresher and helps maintain the vitamins.

Tip: Edible flowersmust be in a good condition. You can usually order them from a specialty greengrocers.

Cream cheese and daisy ciabatta

4 ciabattas
200 g (7 oz) soft (or cream) cheese
2 tbsp mayonnaise
1 tbsp chives, finely chopped
1 tbsp parsley, finely chopped
1 tbsp chervil, finely chopped
1 courgette, in ½ cm (0.2 ") thick slices
2 tbsp olive oil
25 g (3/4 oz) daisy flowers, untreated
salt and freshly ground pepper

1 In a mixing bowl, gently stir the cheese together with the mayonnaise and mix in the herbs. Add a small amount of salt and a generous amount of freshly ground pepper.

2 Heat the grill on the highest setting. Coat the courgette slices with olive oil. Grill the slices for roughly 1 minute on each side.

3 Cut the ciabattas through the middle and spread with the herb and cheese mixture. Place a few grilled courgette slices and some daisies on each ciabatta.

21

Sandwiches

You can turn any 'ordinary' sandwich into something special by just working with it a little. Not enough time? Fresh salads from a specialty cheese shop or greengrocers are much tastier than the pre-packaged stuff from the supermarket. But you can still 'beautify' supermarket salads by adding a couple nice leaves of lettuce or rocket, watercress, alfalfa, fresh herbs, avocado slices, radishes, sweet peppers, grated carrot, slices of pineapple, peaches, strawberries...

If you cut the crust off sandwich bread, then slice the sandwich into strips lengthwise, or diagonally into triangles, or stamp out circles with a biscuit (cookie) cutter, then any old sandwich suddenly becomes a gourmet dish. Cut each sandwich into a different shape depending on the filling.

'Sandwich roll-ups'

With a little more work you can also create clever little 'sandwich roll-ups'. Ask the baker to slice the loaf of bread lengthwise instead of the usual way. This will give you long strips of bread. Just cut off the crust and top the slice with whatever filling you want. Roll it up, starting at one of the short ends. Keep the roll-up somewhere cool, wrapped in plastic wrap, then cut the sandwich into attractive rounds to serve.

Flatbread mega-sandwich

For 8 people

1 round of (Turkish style) flatbread,
cut in half horizontally
4 sweet peppers
200 g (7 oz) garlic salami, sliced
4 tomatoes, sliced
2 red onions, cut into ringlets
50 g (1.75 oz) rocket
100 g (3.5 oz) black olives,
pitted and sliced
200 g (7 oz) feta, sliced
50 g (1.75 oz) cornichons
(miniature gherkins)
pepper

for the tuna mayonnaise:

100 g (3.5 oz) tinned tuna
1 dl (3.5 oz) mayonnaise
2 tbsp crème fraîche
3 sun-dried tomatoes
2 tbsp vinegar from the gherkin jar

1. Roast the peppers for 15-20 minutes in an oven at 220° C (425° F or gas mark 7) or until the outside is blackened. Place them in a closed container or plastic bag to cool. Remove the peel (this should slip right off), the seeds and stem, and slice the peppers into strips.
2. For the tuna mayonnaise, blend all the ingredients in a food processor.
3. Spread the tuna mayonnaise over the bottom half of the flatbread. Top this with the slices of salami, tomato, pepper strips, onion ringlets, rocket, olives, feta and gherkins. Sprinkle with pepper.
4. Close with the top half and press well. Cut the sandwich into pieces to serve.

Tip: You can also use roasted peppers from the jar for this recipe.

23

Multi-grain brown bread

500 g (17.5 oz) all-purpose flour
20 g (0.75 oz) bran
20 g (0.75 oz) wheat germ
20 g (0.75 oz) milled oats
15 g (0.5 oz) malt
12 g (0.5 oz) salt
7 g (0.25 oz) dried yeast, or 15 g (0.5 oz) fresh
300 ml (10.5 oz) lukewarm water

1 Combine the flour, bran, wheat germ, milled oats, malt, salt and dry yeast. (If using fresh yeast, first dissolve it in a small amount of lukewarm water, then add this to the rest of the water.)

2 Add the water and knead until you have a nice smooth dough. Knead for at least 10 minutes.

3 Place the dough in a large mixing bowl and cover. Keep this in a warm place to rise for half an hour or until the dough has doubled in size.

4 Knead the dough once more, shape it into a ball and sprinkle with a little flour.

5 Place the ball of dough on a greased baking sheet and put the whole thing in a plastic bag. Blow the bag up slightly and close it with a clip. (Of course, you can always just put a tea towel over the dough too.) Put in a warm place and let the dough rise another 45 minutes.

6 Preheat the oven to 225° C (435° F or gas mark 7).

7 Remove the baking sheet from the bag, taking care not to touch the dough. Bake for 35 minutes or until cooked through. Immediately remove the bread from the oven and let cool.

Tip: This hearty bread is best cut into thick slices and eaten with some well-aged farm-house cheese (maybe you can even pick some up from a real farm along the way!).

Layered picnic bread

Buy a big round of crusty peasant bread, cut the top off and scoop out the inside until you have a crust about 5 cm (2 ") thick. Fill the bread in layers. Some tasty fillings are, for example, roasted vegetables, crumbled feta and olives; or sun-dried tomatoes, basil and soft, creamy goat's cheese; or tinned tuna, tomatoes, capers and rocket. Press the filling down well, replace the top and wrap the loaf in a tea towel. Cut it into slices to serve.

Breadboxes and biscuit (cookie) barrels

Plastic containers are handy, but there are much more attractive and decorative methods of getting your food from point A to B. Poke around in the attic, at your grandparents' or flea markets for antique breadboxes, old biscuit barrels (cookie jars), pretty tins and attractive old thermoses. Tie the flatware together with lace ribbons or leather cords. A wicker basket is nice for carrying the tablecloths, dishes and flatware (but keep the actual food in an ice box). Plastic tablecloths are handy and quite decorative, available by the piece or in a roll, and in all sorts of colours and special designs. You can even find 'lace' versions now. In certain shops you can also find 'imitation' crystal, made from plastic – non-breakable and certainly less dear than the real stuff. All these elements together will give quite a chic effect!

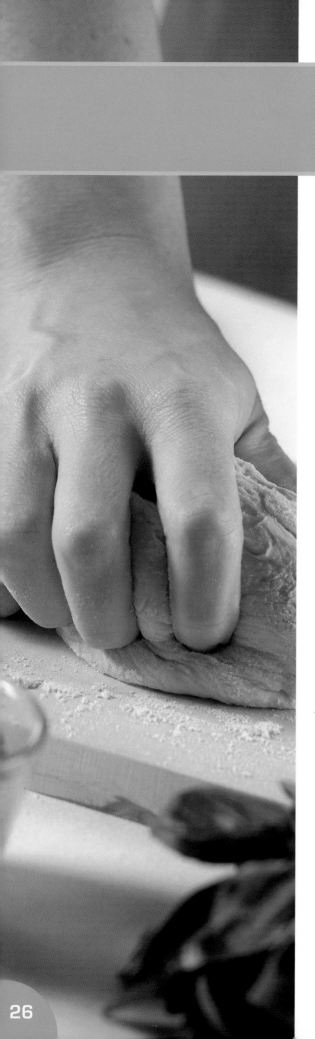

Currant loaf

800 g (28 oz) flour – 25 g (0.9 oz) yeast – 15 g (0.5 oz) salt – 400 ml
(14 oz) milk – 150 g (5.25 oz) currants, soaked in rum or water –
150 g (5.25 oz) raisins, soaked in rum or water – zest (grated rind)
of 1 lemon

1 Combine the flour, yeast and salt and mix well. Add the milk and
   knead to a dough.
2 Knead for 10 minutes, then place the dough in a large mixing bowl.
   Cover it in the currants and raisins and leave it like this to rise for
   30 minutes.
3 Knead the dough once again, making sure to mix in the currants and
   raisins, together with the lemon zest, until evenly distributed.
4 Shape the dough into a roll, place this in a greased bread tin (pan)
   and let this rise another 45 minutes in a warm place, covered.
   Preheat the oven to 225°C (435° F or gas mark 7).
5 Place the bread tin (pan) in the oven and bake for roughly 35 minutes.
   Immediately remove the bread from the oven and let cool.

Chèvre bread

For 15 servings
500 g (17.5 oz) flour
1 tsp salt
2 tbsp coarsely ground
black pepper
1 tbsp sugar
1 egg
60 g (2 oz) softened
butter
150 g (5.25 oz) soft goat's
cheese, crumbled
250 g (8.75 oz) spinach
leaves, chopped
125 ml (4.5 oz)
(goat's) milk
200 ml (7 oz) water

1 In a mixing bowl, combine the flour, salt and pepper and sugar.
2 Stir in the egg and butter.
3 Mix this with the goat's cheese, spinach leaves, milk and water.
4 Knead to a soft and supple dough.
5 Place the dough in a bread tin (pan) and bake at 200° C (400° F or gas mark 6) for 30-35 minutes or until cooked through.
6 Cut the loaf into slices, then the slices into strips.
7 You can serve the bread like this, or toasted.

Turkey, olive and tarragon pasta salad

For 8 people

1 tbsp oil

400 g (14 oz) small noodles, such as conchiglie

400 g (14 oz) turkey fillet

1 tbsp butter

0.5 l (1 pint) chicken stock

3 cloves of garlic, crushed

4 sprigs of tarragon, leaves and stems separate

100 g (3.5 oz) black olives, pitted and finely chopped

3 pink grapefruits, cut into segments
(fresh or from the tin)

1 dl (3.5 oz) cream

4 tbsp mayonnaise

2 tbsp tarragon vinegar

4 tbsp tarragon leaves

salt and pepper

1 Fry the turkey fillet in the butter and oil until brown on each side. Put the meat on a baking sheet, sprinkle with salt and pepper and roast this in the oven for 15 minutes at 180°C (350° F or gas mark 4). Remove from the oven and allow to cool.

2 Bring the chicken stock and 0.5 l (1pint) water to a boil together with the garlic and sprigs of tarragon. Add the pasta and cook until tender. Strain the pasta (save the stock for a soup or other dish) and rinse with cold water. Discard the garlic and sprigs of tarragon.

3 Cut the turkey into cubes and mix these into the cold pasta along with the remaining ingredients. Season the salad with salt and pepper to taste.

Nice cold water

Make sure you bring along plenty of water, especially on hot days. The night before you can fill plastic bottles, one for each person, halfway with water and place these in the freezer. Put them directly into the ice chest when you leave (this way they will also keep the other stuff cold) and fill the bottles to the top with more water at the last minute.

Tip: This salad is also delicious hot, as a snack or tapa.

Chic peas and prawns

1 500 g (17.5 oz) tin of chic peas, drained
150 g (5.25 oz) prawns, peeled
olive oil
1 red onion, thinly sliced
½ red pepper, finely chopped
1 clove of garlic, chopped
1 bay leaf
1 beefsteak tomato, peeled and diced
1-2 tbsp fresh coriander (cilantro), chopped
salt

1 Gently sauté the onion in a dash of olive oil until translucent.
2 Briefly sauté the red pepper, garlic and bay with the onion.
3 Add the chic peas and tomatoes and simmer this mixture for 5 minutes.
4 Add the coriander and prawns and heat through well. Salt to taste.
5 Serve warm or cold with toast.

On the water, in the woods, at the beach, on the heath, in the park... Seek out a good spot in advance of the picnic and come up with some activities that are sure to stimulate the appetite, such as a hike, bicycle ride or boat trip. Get a detailed map of the area from the tourist board. If you opt for a hike, begin and end at the spot where you plan on eating, so that you can leave everything in the car. If you're bicycling, make sure everything fits in the saddlebags or on the rear rack.

Food safety

It's very important to keep food cool, as this is the best protection against the growth of bacteria. Make sure the ice box is kept as cold as possible; you can do this by first chilling salads, sandwiches and the like before putting them in the box. Wait until you're nearly out of the door to move things from the refrigerator into the ice box). Try to find a spot with a little shade so that the food does not have to sit out in the full sun. Whatever the circumstances, nothing should be left unrefrigerated for more than an hour. It's

To the great outdoors!

best to throw out any leftovers that have spent too much time in the sun. You have to be especially careful with mayonnaise-based sauces, as these spoil faster than dressings made from oil and vinegar.

A nice cool red

Sparkling wine tastes wonderfully festive with all sorts of sand-wiches and gourmet snacks. Just like a cool, dry blush wine, 'bubbly' goes great with savoury egg dishes like frittata or sal-mon quiche. But don't be afraid to opt for a young, fruity red wine like Beaujolais for your picnic. Take the bottle along in an ice box (chest), making sure you remove it in plenty of time to reach the right temperature – it should be cool, not ice-cold. Other light red wines are also well suited to drinking cooled. Pick out a soft, fruity wine from South Africa or Chile, for in-stance, or an early Italian.

Tip: Cut the frittata into single servings at home and pack these up in aluminium foil. This makes it easier to transport and dish up.

Feta, cherry tomato and rocket frittata

for 8 people – 8 eggs - 2 dl (7 oz) cream - 1 tbsp butter - 100 g (3.5 oz) feta, crumbled - 1 pint cherry tomatoes, halved - 8 rocket leaves

1 Whisk the eggs together with the cream and add salt and pepper.
2 Heat the butter in a frying pan, not hot enough to actually brown it.
3 Turn the heat down low and pour in the egg mixture.
4 Sprinkle the feta and cherry tomatoes over the egg.
5 Keep on low heat for about 45 minutes or until cooked through. Add the rocket and cook for another 5 minutes.

400 g (14 oz) smoked salmon,
coarsely chopped
125 g (4.5 oz) butter, in small cubes
250 g (1 cup) flour
1 tbsp cold water
1 egg
1 tsp salt
butter for greasing,
or baking paper
1 onion, finely chopped
3 tbsp butter
2 tbsp chives, finely chopped
1 clove of garlic, finely chopped
250 g (8.75 oz) frozen spinach,
drained
5 eggs
2.5 dl (1 cup) milk
2.5 dl (1 cup) whipping cream
pepper

Smoked salmon quiche

1 Press the pieces of butter together with the flour until they resemble fine breadcrumbs. Add water, egg and salt and knead to an even dough.

2 Shape 2/3 of the dough into a round ball, press this slightly flat, then cover it in plastic film (wrap). Repeat with the remaining dough. Keep the balls of dough in the refrigerator for 1 hour to set.

3 Preheat the oven to 160° C (325° F or gas mark 3). Take the dough out of the fridge and roll the larger ball out to a round sheet large enough to cover a springform baking tin (pan) of 24 cm (9.5 ") Repeat with the smaller ball (this sheet will be used for the top of the quiche). Grease the pan with butter or cover with baking paper.

4 Sauté the onion in the butter until it appears translucent. Add the salmon, chives, garlic and spinach, turn off the heat and allow the mixture to cool down.

5 Cover the bottom of the pan with the salmon mixture. Beat the eggs together with the milk, whipping cream and pepper. Pour this over the salmon.

6 Cover the quiche with the second round of dough. Press the edges of the two sheets together until tight. Bake for 30 minutes or until golden brown and cooked through.

for 12 pieces – 250 g (8.75 oz) small sausages, sliced – 2 tbsp olive oil – 1 shallot, minced – 1 potato, diced – 1 celery stalk, sliced into half-moons, 1 pear, grated –100 g (3.5 oz) Stilton, crumbled – 2 tbsp fresh parsley, finely chopped – 1 tbsp Worcestershire sauce – 12 sheets of puff pastry, defrosted- butter for greasing – 3 eggs – 3 tbsp cream – 150 g (5.25 oz) cheese, grated – salt and pepper

Sausage and Stilton mini-quiches

1 Heat the olive oil and fry the sausages, shallot, potato and celery on medium heat for 15 minutes.
2 Transfer to a bowl and allow to cool. Stir in the pear, stilton and parsley and season with Worcestershire sauce, add salt and pepper to taste.
3 Stamp small rounds out of the puff pastry sheets the right size to fit in muffin pans and place these rounds in the greased pans. Divide the sausage mixture over the top.
4 Whisk the eggs together with the cream and add salt and pepper to taste. Divide this over the sausage mixture. Sprinkle with the grated cheese.
5 Bake the mini-quiches for 25 minutes at 200° C (400° F or gas mark 6) or until golden brown and cooked through.

Chicken salad

For 10 servings
200 g (7 oz) chicken fillet,
in small cubes
300 g (10.5 oz) potatoes,
boiled and cut into small cubes
1 onion, cut into small chunks
1 clove of garlic, pressed
1 tbsp red wine vinegar
1 tsp capers
1 avocado, cut into small chunks
2 tomatoes, cut into small chunks
½ bunch radishes, halved
3 tbsp green olives,
coarsely chopped
salt and pepper
olive oil
mayonnaise

1 Fry the chicken fillet in olive oil for 5 minutes or until cooked through. Turn off the heat and allow to cool.
2 In a mixing bowl, combine the onion, garlic, vinegar, capers, avocado, tomatoes, radishes and olives.
3 Add the potatoes and chicken fillet and stir well to mix all the ingredients. Stir in salt, pepper and mayonnaise to taste. Serve at room temperature.

500 g (17.5 oz)
asparagus,
boiled and cut into
segments
1 tbsp chervil,
coarsely chopped
1 tbsp parsley,
coarsely chopped
1 tbsp watercress,
chopped
100 g (3.5 oz) lamb's
lettuce
12 cherry tomatoes,
halved
100 g (3.5 oz)
Parmesan cheese,
in thin curls

For the dressing:
2 tbsp olive oil
2 tbsp lemon juice
sea salt

Tip: Keep the dressing in a separate container and drizzle it on at the very last moment. This will keep the lettuce leaves nice and crisp.

Herb salad with asparagus and Parmesan

1 Combine the oil, lemon juice and a little sea salt.
2 Toss the herbs and lettuce with the dressing.
3 Arrange the asparagus over the salad and garnish with the cheese and tomatoes.

For 4-6 people
1 cantaloupe
2 pears
2 apples
3 oranges,
peel and pith removed
and the fruit cut into
segments
400 ml (14 oz) Spumante
or other sweet sparkling
wine
8 sprigs of mint, leaves

Fruit salad with orange

1 Cut the melon, pears and apples into segments and remove the peels, seeds and core.
2 Cut the segments into triangles.
3 Slice off the top and bottom of the orange peel. Place the oranges right-side-up and, using a good sharp knife, cut the remaining peel off from top to bottom, including the inner white pith, which is bitter, until you are left with only the fruit. Using a paring knife, cut out the individual segments. Make sure you catch all the juice, this should not go to waste.
4 Marinade the fruit for 1 hour together with the Spumante, orange and mint.

Yoghurt pancakes

125 g (4.5 oz) flour
5 tbsp orange juice
1 egg
1 tbsp sugar
200 ml (7 oz) yoghurt
4 tbsp butter, melted
butter for frying
salt

1 Combine the flour, orange juice, egg, sugar, yoghurt and salt.
2 Mix in the melted butter.
3 Melt some butter in a heated pan.
4 Make pancakes roughly 7 cm (2.75 ") in diameter with 2 tbsp of batter for each one.
5 Cook until brown and stiff.

Tip: serve the pancakes with extra thick yoghurt and fresh fruit.

37

Lemon tart

Lemon tart

For the base:
1 packet Bastogne biscuits
(or graham crackers),
finely ground in a food processor
1 tbsp lemon marmalade
50 g (1.75 oz) butter

For the filling:
juice of 3 lemons
10 gelatine sheets, soaked in cold water
400 g (14 oz) cream cheese
500 ml (17.5 oz) full-fat yoghurt
100 g (3.5 oz) confectioner's sugar
1 packet vanilla sugar

For the lemon slices:
1 lemon, thinly sliced
1.5 dl (5.25 oz) water
300 g (10.5 oz) sugar

1 For the base, melt the butter and mix with the marmalade and ground biscuits.
2 Cover a springform cake tin with plastic film (wrap) and coat the bottom with the biscuit mixture. Press well.
3 For the lemon slices, bring the water and sugar to a boil on high heat and boil until the mixture clarifies.
4 Turn the heat down low and add the slices of lemon. Simmer these gently in the syrup for 30 minutes. The mixture should not boil.
5 Remove the slices from the syrup with a spatula or slotted spoon and allow to cool.
6 For the filling, heat the lemon juice and dissolve the drained gelatin in this.
7 Combine the cream cheese, yoghurt, confectioner's sugar and vanilla sugar and stir in the lemon juice and gelatin mixture
8 Pour the filling into the cake tin, smooth out the top and place in the refrigerator for 4 hours to set.
9 Arrange the lemon slices over the top and cut the tart into 8 equal pieces.

Tip: Leave the tart in the springform tin and cover it with plastic film (wrap) so that it's easy to transport. It should stay quite cool.

Barbecues

They are becoming increasingly popular, those little portable gas grills. You can also find disposable coal-fired barbecue grills which are easy to ignite. This will make your picnic quite posh! The disposable kind do not burn that long (usually less than is indicated on the package), so don't try grilling a complete meal for eight people on one of these. The grill is more a way of making a few hot snacks to compliment the meal's main course, which should consist of cold dishes. Pre-cooked meat is ideal (especially as a health issue!). Or you can choose from the dishes described in the barbecuing chapter. (But be careful here, because you can't grill everywhere! There are fire regulations preventing it in many places, though in some parks you can find grills for public use. It's best to find out beforehand!)

Tip 1: Try making this sandwich with banana or pear.
Tip 2: Store the toasted sandwiches in an airtight container, this will keep them crisp.

Currant toastie with apple

2 slices currant loaf
1 tbsp honey
¼ apple, cut into slices

1 Spread the honey onto both slices of bread.
2 Fill with the apple slices.
3 Toast the sandwich in a sandwich press until crispy.

Almond mandarin cookies

1 mandarin orange
(choose one with a nice
fragrant peel)
2 egg whites
300 g (10.5 oz) blanched
almonds,
ground to a powder
225 g (8 oz) sugar
100 g (3.5 oz) sliced
almonds
butter for greasing

1 Scrub the mandarin well and use a grater or zester to cut curlicues out of the peel. Chop these finely.
2 Beat the egg whites until stiff and mix in the almond powder, mandarin zest and sugar in increments. The mixture should be stiff but a little light and airy as well.
3 Shape round cookies and dip these into the almond slices until covered.
4 Place on the buttered baking sheet.
5 Bake the cookies in a preheated oven at 200° C (400° F or gas mark 6) for 10-15 minutes or until light brown and cooked through. Immediately remove them from the baking sheet and let them cool to harden.

Multi-purpose serviette
Try using chequered tea towels as serviettes. They look nice and are also big enough to spread out on the ground in place of a plate or place mat. They are also handy for rolling up fragile items for safe transport. Or try making a little bundle out of each one, so that each person has their own wooden board with a plate, flatware and a (plastic) glass wrapped up inside.

Apple lime tart

Apple lime tart

1 kg (2.2 lbs) apples (Gold-Rennet,
Jonagold or Golden Delicious)
peeled and cut into wedges
300 g (10.5 oz) flour
150 g (5.25 oz) white castor sugar
225 g (8 oz) softened butter
pinch of salt
1 egg, beaten
zest (grated rind) of 1 lime
juice of ½ a lime
3 tbsp sugar
1 tsp cinnamon
2 tbsp bread crumbs
butter for greasing

1 Preheat the oven to 175 °C (335° F or gas mark 3).
Combine the flour, sugar, butter, salt and ½ the
beaten egg and knead to a soft dough. Roll out
²/₃ of the dough on a floured surface until you have
a 30 cm (12 ") sheet.

2 Cover the bottom and sides of a greased springform
cake tin with the dough.

3 Combine the apples, lime zest, lime juice, sugar
and cinnamon. Sprinkle the bread crumbs over the
bottom and scoop the filling into the pie pan.

4 Roll out the remaining dough and cut it into 1 cm
(0.4") thick strips. Lay the strips crosswise over the
apple filling.

5 Combine the remaining egg with one tablespoon of
water and brush the tart with the mixture. Sprinkle
with extra sugar and cinnamon if desired, then bake
the tart for 45 minutes or until cooked through.

6 Remove from the oven and allow to cool before
removing from the tin.

500 g (17.5 oz) white
chocolate
500 ml (1 pint) cream,
whipped until half-stiff
2 egg whites
1.5 dl (5.25 oz) cream
4 passion fruits

White chocolate mousse with passion fruit

1 Beat the egg whites until very stiff. Heat the cream and add the chocolate to this to melt.

2 Allow to cool slightly, then mix in the whipped cream.

3 Carefully fold in the egg whites.

4 Divide over 4 glasses and keep in the refrigerator for at least 4 hours to set.

5 Halve the passion fruits through the middle and scoop out the pulp.

6 Remove the glasses from the refrigerator and top with the passion fruit.

Cranberry muffins

For 12 muffins
250 g (8 oz)(1 cup) flour
200 g (7 oz) sugar
2 tsp baking powder
½ tsp salt
3 eggs (medium size)
100 g (3.5 oz) crème
fraîche
50 g (1.75 oz) butter,
melted
1 tsp lemon zest
(grated rind)
1 tbsp lemon juice
150 g (5.25 oz)
cranberries
confectioner's sugar

For the topping:
1 tsp cinnamon
2 tbsp flour
50 g (1.75 oz) butter
50 g (1.75 oz) brown
sugar

1 Preheat the oven to 200 °C (400° F or gas mark 6). Grease 12 muffin moulds.
2 Sift the flour, sugar, baking powder and salt into a mixing bowl and mix well.
3 In a separate bowl, beat the eggs. Stir the crème fraîche well until it becomes nice and smooth, then add to the eggs, stirring constantly, together with the melted butter, lemon zest and lemon juice.
4 Using a rubber spatula, gently fold the egg mixture into the flour with until the two are just mixed. Fold in the cranberries and pour the batter into the muffin pans.
5 In a food processor, blend the ingredients for the topping until you have a grainy mixture. Arrange this over the muffins.
6 Bake for roughly 20 minutes. They are done when a toothpick inserted in the middle comes out clean.
7 Allow the muffins to cool and serve with confectioner's sugar.

Tip: Instead of cranberries, you can also use blueberries, or pieces of another type of fruit, or even chocolate. For a savoury variation, try using herbs or (goat's) cheese.

Mediterranean picnic

gazpacho (p. 17)

***

prawn ciabattas (p. 19)
feta, cherry tomato and rocket frittata (p. 31)
green salad with vinaigrette

***

lemon tart (p. 39)

Preparation

For the grocery shopping, see the ingredients list accompanying the recipes (p. 17,19 31,39). You will also need: 2 bags of washed mixed greens, olive oil and red wine vinegar. Serve a young Italian red wine or a blush, both chilled, and cold (mineral) water. **One day before:** Make the gazpacho and store it in the refrigerator. Freeze ice cubes and iced water bottles (see p. 28). For the vinaigrette mix 50 ml red wine vinegar with 150 ml extra virgin olive oil, salt and pepper in a plastic soda bottle or sealed plastic container. Pack the picnic basket (use the checklist on p. 19). **Do not forget:** a mixing bowl for tossing the salad and bowls and spoons for the soup.

The day of

Bake the lemon tart and the frittata. Make the prawn filling. **One hour before:** Stuff the ciabattas with the prawn filling. Put the gazpacho in thermoses with ice cubes. Just before you leave the house, put everything in the ice box (chest). Once at the picnic site, all you have to do is toss the salad greens with the vinaigrette.

3x faster

Delegate: have someone else cut vegetables and crumble the feta. **Simplify:** for the gazpacho, go for good-quality tinned tomatoes. Buy pre-cooked king prawns. **Leave out:** replace the gazpacho with ready-made antipasti from the deli or straight from the jar (marinated olives, sun-dried tomatoes, artichoke hearts, roasted vegetables...). Replace the lemon tart with fresh fruit such as oranges and grapes.

Menu 2

Classic English picnic

crunchy chicken sandwich (p. 18)
sausage and Stilton mini-quiches (p. 33)
***
cranberry muffins (p. 45)
***
fruit salad with orange (p. 36)

Preparation

For the grocery shopping, see the ingredients list accompanying the recipes (p. 18, 33, 45, 44, 36). Naturally, you should drink tea with these; herbal tea stays fresh longer than black tea. On really hot days, the iced tea on p. 51 is quite refreshing. A dry sparkling wine is delicious with the savoury sandwiches. **One day before:** Prepare the mousse and put it in the fridge to cool. Freeze ice cubes for the iced tea and put the wine in the fridge. Pack the picnic basket (use the checklist on p. 19).

The day of

Bake the quiches. Make the iced tea and the fruit salad. Get the ingredients ready for the sandwiches. Keep everything in the refrigerator until you're ready to leave. **One hour before:** Make the sandwiches.

3x faster

Delegate: have someone else whip the cream, cut the apples, chop the hazelnuts, etc. **Simplify:** Make sandwiches with cooked fillings. Leave out the quiches and take more sandwiches in place (with different fillings, of course). **Leave out:** Leave out one of the sweet dishes, or make currant toasties instead. Instead of a fruit salad, just take along some apples and pears.

Menu 3

Gone over an hour picnic

Preparation

For any time that the weather is suddenly too nice to stay indoors: choose one impressive dish to make yourself and bulk the meal up with cooked snacks such as grilled marinated chicken wings. (Recipes on p. 23, 50,51)

Also very tasty:

Ready-made quiche and all sorts of salads. For the tropical fruit drink (see p. 50) you will need one honeydew melon per 6 people, one carton of pineapple juice and two limes. Also take lots of fresh fruit along, like mangos and strawberries, which you can rinse and serve on the spot. If you have a hankering for wine, go for a dry blush or a chardonnay.

One hour before:

Have someone pack the picnic basket while you're doing the grocery shopping. Make the sandwich (use peppers from a jar) and put all the food, drinks and plenty of water in an ice box.

The tastiest summer drinks

Thick and velvety smoothies chockfull of fruit for a healthy breakfast drink. Jugs of refreshing home-made iced tea and cold sorbet drinks as the perfect pick-me-up on a hazy summer afternoon. Extra-fresh fruit juices and virgin cocktails at a party or served as a pleasantly surprising aperitif... These exquisite summer drinks are wonderfully suited for any time of day.

Fresh and fruity

With your own mix of freshly pressed (citrus) juices, pureed fruit and fruit juice or fruit nectar from the carton, you can prepare the most delectable drinks. A fresh **tropical fruit drink** for example: put pureed honeydew melon in a glass and add an equal amount of pineapple juice, plus a little dash of lime juice. You can make a sweet and sultry drink with a mix of fresh orange juice, apricot nectar and the juice of ½ a passion fruit per glass.

Smoothies

Smoothies are some of the most velvety, cool and all-round delicious drinks in the world. They can easily be made by first freezing fresh fruit, then pureeing it in a blender. This will give the drink a thick and creamy consistency, often with a bit of foam on top. Sometimes they are also made with yoghurt, which gives the drink a wonderfully fresh and tart flavour, and you are free to throw in whatever flavourings you want, as long as the end result is cool and refreshing (and usually still surprisingly healthy).

To make a **melon-orange smoothie** freeze 400 grams (14 oz) of watermelon, 200 grams (7 oz) honeydew melon and 200 grams (7 oz) of fresh pineapple chunks (keep all this in the freezer for at least 4 hours). Puree these ingredients together with the juice of 4 oranges and a lemon. Strawberry-rhubarb smoothie: combine 100 grams (3.5 oz) of rhubarb chunks with 1 tablespoon sugar and allow to sit for 1 hour, then bring to the boil, remove from the heat and allow to cool. Then mix in 200 grams (7 oz) of strawberries and keep the mixture in the freezer for a few hours. Puree the fruit together with 1 tablespoon of honey and the juice of 1 blood orange, then add 500 ml (1 pint) cold whole milk and puree this until it starts to foam.

Mocktails

A lip-smacking, festive cocktail does not always need to be alcoholic. You can mix delicious *and* nutritious drinks using all sorts of fruit juices, sodas and even herbs. Virgin cocktails are sometimes called 'mocktails'. An 'After Midnight' is made by stirring raspberry syrup in a large wine glass with ice cubes and 4 tablespoons of lemon juice. Top off with sparkling mineral water.

Fire & water

A 'fire & water' cocktail is hot and cold at the same time, a wonderfully surprising pick-me-up. You start this cocktail by first making chili syrup: in a small pot, dissolve 100 g (3.5 oz) of sugar in 100 ml (3.5 oz) of water, add a red chili pepper and simmer on low heat to infuse (the longer you keep it on the heat, the spicier the syrup will be). Remove from the heat and allow to cool. Put one tablespoon of the syrup in a blender together with 250 g (8.75 oz) of watermelon, in chunks, and three ice cubes. Garnish with mint leaves and a slice of lime.

Rose and lemon sorbet

Sorbet drinks are just as easy to make with ready-bought fruit sorbets topped off with sparkling mineral water or soda. Take this rose and lemon sorbet, for example: put a scoop of lemon sorbet in a glass, add a dash of rosewater and a spoonful of confectioner's sugar and top off with mineral water. Garnish with unblemished rose petals.

Iced tea can be made by brewing extra-strong tea, which is then cooled and diluted with (sparkling) mineral water. You can add all sorts of seasonings, such as herbs and fruit juices.

Green iced tea with ginger and lemongrass is deliciously refreshing and savoury. Infuse slices of fresh ginger and a stalk of lemongrass, halved lengthwise, in the tea as it steeps, then remove when cool. Add sugar to taste and serve over plenty of ice cubes.

Virgin Mary

There's nothing wrong with serving non-alcoholic versions of famous cocktails, such as this 'Virgin Mary', which is simply a Bloody Mary without the alcohol. In a shaker, mix 80 ml (2.8 oz) tomato juice with a squirt of fresh lime juice, a few drops of Tabasco and Worcestershire sauce, salt and pepper. For a virgin Mojito (p. 147), simply leave out the rum and, if desired, substitute tonic for the mineral water. Above all: use your imagination!

lunch

Big Sunday Lunch

The greatest moment of the week? Sunday afternoon! Finally, the week's stress is over and now you have time for a nice, big, leisurely lunch with your friends. One that seems to go on all afternoon because you can forget all about the time and just enjoy life.

Has life been so hectic recently that you haven't even managed to set a date for a nice, relaxing evening with your friends? There's a good chance that a big Sunday lunch will fit into everyone's schedule. Nobody should have any work or other obligations to fulfil, so you'll all have the whole afternoon to yourselves. And you don't have to worry about finding a babysitter, because the kids can come along too.

The ultimate garden lunch

By 'lunch' we don't mean just a few sandwiches in the back garden. This lunch has at least three courses: a classic creamy asparagus soup, sophisticated seafood starters, a delicious pasta dish, a light main course with crisp stir-fried vegetables... all served with the appropriate wines. In fact, you can pick out any dish you want, but be sure not to make the meal too heavy. Avoid overly filling meat dishes with cream sauces and the like. It's on those hot summer days in particular that people crave light and delicate dishes, fresh salads, cold soups, etc. If you plan on eating with the kids, go for 'child-friendly' foods like oven-roasted chicken, plenty of fresh fruit juice, and a nice, sweet ice cream cone, of course!

Plan flexibly

With a little luck you can celebrate Easter outside with a tasty lunch or a more traditional Easter brunch. Officially, it's brunch if you start eating around eleven o'clock. A luxurious lunch usually kicks off around one or one-thirty. It honestly does not matter all that much: just serve a tasty snack or starter as soon as people start getting hungry. The main course can already be prepared, so that you're free to decide when to serve it. Flexible planning can definitely come in handy when you have the garden full of people relaxing from their week and children running about...

Summer lunch

Scampi with mango salad

16 large scampi tails with the shell
4 lime slices
mint leaves for garnishing

For the salad:
2 mangos, cut into small strips
2 Spanish red peppers, deseeded,
cut into thin strips
3 shallots, sliced paper-thin
2 tbsp mint leaves, chopped
2 heaping tbsp garden cress or daikon cress

For the dressing:
1 tsp sea salt
2 tbsp fresh coriander (cilantro)
2 green peppers,
deseeded and finely chopped
3 tbsp Thai fish sauce
4 tbsp brown or palm sugar
4 tbsp lemon juice

1 Make the dressing: blend all the ingredients in a food processor until you have a sauce of even consistency. Taste, adding more salt if necessary.
2 In a large mixing bowl, combine all the ingredients for the salad and add the dressing.
3 Fry or grill the scampi on high heat until cooked through.
4 Arrange the salad on the plates and top with the scampi. Garnish with a slice of lime and mint leaves if desired.

Avocado salad with oranges and cashews

2 ripe avocados, thinly sliced
2 oranges
50 g (1.75 oz) cashews
2 eggs, hardboiled for 5 minutes,
then peeled and mashed
1/2 tbsp white wine vinegar
2 tbsp nut oil
juice of 1 lemon
50 g (1.75 oz) mixed lettuce
4 tbsp crème fraîche
salt and pepper

1 Remove the peel and white pith from the oranges. Separate the segments, capturing the juice.
2 Combine the vinegar, oil, lemon and orange juice. Add salt and pepper to taste. Toss with the lettuce.
3 Arrange the lettuce over the plates. Top with the crème fraîche and the slices of avocado and orange. Sprinkle with the nuts and hardboiled egg. Add a little salt to taste.

Tip: Avocados go brown extremely fast once cut. You can keep them looking fresh longer with a little lemon juice or vinegar.

Radicchio salad with bacon dressing

1 head of radicchio, cut into thin strips
4 heads of endive, leaves only
1 bunch of watercress, stemmed
2 firm ripe pears,
peeled and cut lengthwise into thin slices

For the dressing:
100 g (3.5 oz) bacon, very finely diced
8 tbsp olive oil
0.5 dl (1.75 oz) balsamic vinegar
1 tbsp brown sugar
1 tbsp soy sauce
50 g (1.75 oz) raisins, finely chopped

1 For the dressing, fry the diced bacon in 1 tbsp of oil on low heat. When the meat has crisped up, add the vinegar, sugar and soy sauce and stir well until the sugar is completely dissolved.

2 Add the chopped raisins and the rest of the oil, remove from the heat and let the dressing cool.

3 Arrange the lettuce, endive and watercress on plates together with the pear slices, then drizzle with the dressing.

Stir-fried spring vegetables

2-3 tbsp butter
12 small shallots, peeled
12 small cloves of garlic
12 pieces of green onion
12 radishes + the leaves
24 wild spinach leaves
1 tbsp dry mustard
2 tbsp castor sugar
1 dl (3.5 oz) white wine
12 pieces of fennel
12 button mushrooms
12 pieces of carrot, blanched
pint of garden cress

1 In a wok, fry the shallots and garlic with butter until slightly brown.
2 Add the green onion, radish leaves and spinach.
3 Combine the dry mustard, sugar and white wine. Pour this into the hot vegetable mixture in the wok and continue cooking for 1 minute.
4 Add the fennel, mushrooms, radishes and carrot to the wok and cook a further 3 minutes.
5 Sprinkle with the garden cress and serve.

Focaccia with cheese and dried tomatoes

400 g (14 oz) wheat flour, sifted – 1 tsp salt – 14 g (0.5 oz) dried yeast – 1 tbsp sugar – 20 g (0.7 oz) butter, softened – 200 ml (7 oz) hot water – olive oil – 1 mozzarella ball, sliced – 100 g (3.5 oz) dried tomatoes – 4 sprigs of rosemary – coarse sea salt

1 Mix the flour with the salt, then add the yeast.
2 Mix the sugar with the butter and water.
3 Add the sugar mixture to the flour and knead for a few minutes until you have an even dough.
4 Cover and put in a warm place to rise; allow to rise until the dough has doubled in size.
5 Divide it into two pieces. Roll the dough out to 2 round sheets, each 1 cm (0.4 ") thick.
6 Place 1 sheet on a greased baking tray and arrange the cheese and tomato over the top. Top with the second sheet of dough, pressing the edges firmly together. Brush the top with olive oil, sprinkle with rosemary and sea salt and allow to rise another 30 minutes. Preheat the oven to 200° C (400° F, gas mark 6).
7 Bake for 20 minutes or until golden brown. As soon as it comes out of the oven, brush it immediately with olive oil and let cool.

Tip: You can make all sorts of other fillings for this dish as well; try olives and basil, thyme, Parmesan cheese, nuts... And fresh focaccia is even delicious on its own without any filling!

Classic asparagus soup

500 g (17.5 oz) white asparagus, peeled (save the peels), and sliced into diagonal pieces
1 l (1 qt) beef bouillon
40 g (1.4 oz) butter
35 g (1.25 oz) flour
2 dl (7 oz) cream
salt

1 Steep the asparagus peels in the bouillon for 10 minutes. Strain the bouillon and set aside to cool.
2 Make a roux: melt the butter, stir in the flour and cook until the colour deepens somewhat.
3 Add a soup spoon of cold bouillon and stir until the flour is well mixed with the bouillon. Add some more bouillon and continue in this manner until all the bouillon has been absorbed.
4 Briefly bring the soup to a boil, then strain to remove any remaining lumps.
5 Heat the soup through well once more, then add the cream and the pieces of asparagus and allow to steep until the asparagus is just tender.
6 Add salt to taste.

Tip: Always keep the bouillon just on the verge of a boil: if the asparagus or asparagus peel is boiled too vigorously, they develop a bitter taste.

Easter in style

If you want to create a modern and stylish Easter spread, then keep it sleek and easy. You can do this, for example, by arranging two glass jars on the table and filling them with white or brown eggs (hard-boiled, to make them safe and edible). Or place a few vases on the table with spring branches; these will be real eye-catchers. Keep the colour scheme subdued, using more browns and whites.

Easter fresh

If you want to bring a little more colour to the table, go for yellow – this is the traditional Easter colour, after all. Spread the colour around in all different hues, from soft pastel to bright yellow or ochre. Complement these with pure whites and you will have a beautiful, spring-fresh Easter spread. And not just for Easter: just pick out your favourite colour for a lovely spring or summer table decoration.

Happy Easter

If a lot of children are coming over for lunch, you can let them help out by making amusing Easter decorations. Stuff a few coloured chocolate eggs into a flower arrangement, for instance. If you stick them on skewers, you can place them at various heights about the flowers for a pretty, playful effect. Or turn empty eggs into inventive candles: take the wicks out of tea lights and place them in the eggshell halves, melt the candle wax in a double boiler and carefully pour this into the eggs until the wick sticks far enough out to light. This looks especially nice if you put the shells back into the egg carton – they will stay upright and won't make such a mess!

1 kg (2.2 lbs) shellfish (mussels
and clams)
4 tbsp unsalted butter
100 g (3.5 oz) bacon,
in small cubes
200 g (7 oz) onions, thinly sliced
100 g (3.5 oz) celery, sliced
50 g (1.75 oz) carrots,
thinly sliced
1.2 l (1.25 qts) chicken stock
1 tsp thyme, leaves only
1 tsp dried oregano
2 tins peeled Italian tomatoes
(+/- 400 g (14 oz)),
drained and chopped
2 medium-sized potatoes,
diced
1 tbsp orange zest (grated
orange rind)
salt and freshly ground pepper,
to taste

Shellfish and vegetable soup

1 In a large pot, melt the butter and fry the bacon until cooked through. Add the onion and celery and sauté another 10 minutes.

2 Add the remaining ingredients (except the shellfish and the orange zest) and simmer for roughly 30 minutes on low heat, covered.

3 Meanwhile, scrub the mussels and clams clean and put them in a pan (pot) with a little water. Cover the pan (pot) and steam the shellfish until they are all open. Pour them into a colander and strain well. Discard any shells which did not open.

4 Taste the soup, adding salt and pepper to taste. Add the shellfish just before serving, simmer them in the soup for a minute to heat them through.

5 Serve the soup in warm bowls and garnish with the orange zest.

Danish cheese and celery soup

60 g (2 oz) Danish blue
cheese
50 g (1.75 oz) butter
2 medium-sized onions,
finely chopped
1 bunch of celery,
rinsed and thinly sliced
30 g (1 oz) flour
1 l (1 qt) chicken stock
1 tbsp parsley,
finely chopped
salt and pepper

1 Melt the butter and sauté the onion and celery for 10 minutes, without browning.
2 Stir the flour into the vegetables and continue sautéing a few minutes longer.
3 Stirring constantly, add the bouillon, cover the soup and simmer for 40 minutes or until the celery has become thoroughly soft.
4 Finely crumble the cheese and stir in a small bowl until softened. Just before serving, mix the cheese into the soup. Do not allow the soup to come to a boil after this point. Add salt and pepper to taste and garnish with parsley.

Tip: Instead of Danish Blue you can also use a blue cheese with a milder flavour.

Cold courgette and cumin soup

500 g (17.5 oz) courgette, cut into small chunks
1 tbsp olive oil
1 large onion, finely chopped
1 celery stalk, sliced
1 tsp ground cumin
1 l (1 qt) chicken stock
1 large bunch fresh basil, a few leaves set aside for garnish, the rest finely chopped
2 tbsp soft, or cream, cheese
salt and pepper

1 Heat the oil in a pan (pot) on medium heat. Add the onion and celery and sauté for about 15 minutes or until the onion is translucent.
2 Add the cumin and cook for about 30 seconds longer.
3 Stir in the courgette and add the chicken stock. Bring the soup to a boil, turn the heat to low and simmer for about 30 minutes or until the courgette is thoroughly softened. Set aside to cool.
4 Mix the chopped basil into the soup. Puree the soup in batches in the blender until it has a nice smooth consistency, then pour into a serving bowl. Add salt and pepper to taste. Cover the bowl and place the soup in the refrigerator for 3 hours to chill (this soup can be made 1 day in advance if kept overnight in the refrigerator).
5 Ladle the soup into small bowls. Serve with a scoop of soft, or cream, cheese and the remaining basil leaves.

Tip: Because this soup is served chilled, it should be fully seasoned first. Cumin provides a very full and rich flavour, though the soup still requires a good deal of black pepper to round it off.

Fettuccine with sage and chèvre

500 g (17.5 oz) fettuccine
4 tbsp olive oil or butter
200 g (7 oz) freshly grated aged
goat's cheese (chèvre)
freshly grated black pepper to taste
sea salt

1   In a large pan (pot), bring 6 litres of water to
    a boil, adding 3 tablespoons of sea salt when
    boiling.
2   Drop in the pasta and boil for roughly 4 minutes
    or until tender (or follow the instructions on the
    package).
3   Fry the sage leaves in the olive oil until crispy.
    Remove and let the oil drain, then sprinkle
    with salt.
4   Strain the pasta and toss with the oil and half the
    grated cheese.
5   Divide the pasta over the plates and sprinkle the
    remaining cheese, fried sage leaves and ground
    black pepper over the top.

Tip 1: Delicious with sereh sauce.
Tip 2: Cut the red bream into smaller pieces (200 g for 8 pieces) and you have the perfect cocktail snack (you can leave off the sauce for this).

Red bream with crispy bacon

400 g (14 oz) fillets of red bream, 8 pieces
1 bunch basil
8 large slices of bacon
olive oil

1 Preheat the oven to 160 °C (325° F or gas mark 3). Place a basil leaf on each piece of fish and roll these up in the bacon slices.

2 Place the pieces of red bream in a baking dish, drizzle with a bit of olive oil and cook for roughly 15 minutes or until heated through.

Sereh sauce

200 ml (7 oz) fish jus
100 ml (3.5 oz) white wine
100 ml (3.5 oz) cream
1 lemongrass (sereh) stalk, cut into large segments

First make the sauce: bring all the ingredients to a boil, reduce to half (or less, if you prefer it somewhat thicker) and taste to adjust for salt and pepper.

Yoghurt-glazed fish fillets

4 fish fillets, such as salmon trout or cod - 1 egg white, beaten stiff -
1 dl (3.5 oz) yoghurt - 1 tbsp dill, very finely chopped - 4 tbsp bread crumbs -
8 cherry tomatoes - salt and freshly ground pepper

1 Combine the beaten egg white with the yoghurt and dill.
2 Sprinkle the fillets with salt and pepper and cover with the yoghurt. Do not use all the yoghurt.
3 Sprinkle with the bread crumbs and place the fillets in a greased baking dish.
4 Slice the cherry tomatoes in half lengthwise and mix with the remaining yoghurt.
5 Arrange these around the fish fillets and place on the middle of the broiler rack.
6 Broil the fish for 10-14 minutes or until crispy and cooked through.

Colourful place mats

You can easily create a certain atmosphere or style with your table by decorating with place mats or table runners. Make them, say, from groovy '70s-style wallpaper in fresh summer colours. You can buy this by the roll and immediately have an attractive eye-catcher on the table. The tone is set, you don't need much more ornamentation! Or you can make them from linen in one or two colours. Cut them out into nice even shapes and unravel about an inch on each end by pulling the threads out a bit. A pleasant effect for which no sewing machine is needed. Table runners can also be placed crosswise over the table, so that two people sitting across from each other are connected by the fabric.

Table moods

Skin-fried cod

4 cod fillets, each 100 g (3.5 oz), skin on
2 sweet red peppers
200 g (7 oz) coarsely chopped spinach leaves
1 tbsp olive oil (for sautéing)
sea salt
freshly grated pepper

For the dressing:
4 tbsp olive oil
4 tbsp balsamic vinegar

1 Roast the peppers at 220° C (425° F or gas mark 7) for roughly 35 minutes or until blackened.

2 Remove from the oven, cover and allow to cool (about 10 minutes), then remove the charred peel, the stem and seeds and cut into large pieces.

3 Sauté the pepper pieces in 1 tablespoon of olive oil in a hot frying pan, then place them on warm plates.

4 Heat a frying pan on a high heat. When hot, drop in the butter and oil and fry the cod skin-side-down for roughly 7 minutes or until golden brown and cooked through.

5 Place the fish on top of the pepper pieces.

6 In the same pan, briefly wilt the washed spinach. Arrange the chopped spinach beside the cod and peppers.

7 For the dressing, combine the olive oil and balsamic vinegar. Briefly warm the dressing in a saucepan and drizzle it from a tablespoon over and around the cod. Season with sea salt and freshly grated pepper.

Lamb chops with vegetables

4 lamb chops, 200 g (7 oz) each
1 bulb garlic
5 tbsp olive oil
600 g (21 oz) floury cooking potatoes, peeled
4 tomatoes, sliced
2 courgettes, sliced
2 sprigs of thyme, leaves only
generous dash of milk
25 g (0.9 oz) butter
salt and pepper

1 Preheat the oven to 175 °C (335° F or gas mark 3). Slice the top off the garlic bulb and place the bulb on a piece of aluminium foil. Sprinkle with salt and 2 tablespoons of olive oil, then wrap it tightly in the foil. Bake for roughly 1 hour.

2 Boil the potatoes.

3 Spread the tomato courgette slices domino-style in circles on a baking sheet. Drizzle with 2 tablespoons of olive oil and sprinkle with a little sea salt, pepper and thyme. Bake for roughly 4 minutes at 175° C (335° F or gas mark 3).

4 In 1 tablespoons of oil, fry the lamb until brown on each side, seasoning with salt and pepper as it cooks. Place the lamb chops in a baking dish and bake for 5 minutes or until hot through.

5 Meanwhile, scoop the softened garlic pulp out of the bulb and mash this with the potatoes and a little milk and butter (or olive oil if you prefer) until you have a light puree.

6 Serve the courgette and tomato rounds on a layer of mashed potatoes and top with the sliced lamb.

Provençal tart with sweet pepper sauce

2 small aubergines, thinly sliced - 400 g (14 oz) spinach - 250 g (8.75 oz) soft goat's cheese, sliced - 100 g (3.5 oz) hazelnuts, finely chopped - 3 tbsp olive oil **For the sauce:** - 4 sweet red peppers, in pieces - 1 onion - 8 cloves of garlic, minced – 1 tbsp tomato puree – 4 dl (14 oz) vegetable stock - ½ bunch of basil, very finely chopped – ½ bunch of thyme, leaves very finely chopped - salt and pepper

1 For the sauce, heat 1 tbsp oil and sauté the pepper, onion and 6 cloves of garlic. Stir in the tomato puree and continue cooking briefly. Pour in the stock and add the herbs.
2 Simmer for roughly 15 minutes, then puree with a hand-held blender until you have a chunky sauce. Add salt and pepper to taste.
3 In 1 tablespoon of oil, fry the aubergine until nice and brown on each side.
4 In 1 tablespoon oil, stir-fry the spinach with 2 cloves of garlic until wilted.
5 Place 4 cooking rings on plates, one per plate, and fill each one successively with slices of aubergine, spinach, half the goat's cheese and nuts, the sweet pepper sauce (set half of this aside) and finish with the remaining cheese and nuts.
6 Bake the tarts for roughly 15 minutes at 175° C (335° F or gas mark 3).
7 Heat the remaining sauce and ladle this around the tarts. Remove the rings.

Tip: Make sure you use heat-resistant plates. Otherwise, use small casserole dishes or ramekins.

Dips and spreads

It's nice to have something ready for your guests to snack on as they arrive. One easy dish to keep them going is **hummus**, a splendid Middle Eastern chic pea puree. In a food processor or mortar and pestle, puree one can of chic peas together with two cloves of garlic, the juice of one lemon, salt to taste, a dash of olive oil and two tablespoons tahini (sesame butter) until you have a smooth mixture. Put the hummus in an attractive serving dish and sprinkle a little paprika or chili powder and some chopped parsley over the top. This makes a great dip for pita points or wedges of flatbread.

You can also make one or more of the pestos and tapenades described on p. 150. Spread them on some nice, crisp **crostini**: to make these, cut a baguette into thin slices on the diagonal, brush each slice on both sides with olive oil and sprinkle with a little coarse sea salt. Bake at 200° C (400° F or gas mark 6) for about five minutes or until they are golden brown. Keep the crostini in a biscuit jar until ready to serve.

Free-range chicken with lemon

1 whole free-range chicken, approx.
1.5 kg (3.3 lbs)
2 lemons
1 bunch of tarragon
1 red chilli pepper, finely chopped
2 cloves of garlic, peeled and
Finely chopped
8 tbsp olive oil
salt and freshly ground pepper

1 Preheat the oven to 200 °C (400° F or gas mark 6).

2 Mix 2 tablespoons of olive oil with a generous amount of salt and freshly ground pepper. Brush the cavity of the chicken with this mixture.

3 Stuff the bird with half the bunch of tarragon, half the red chili pepper and half the garlic. Finally, insert one lemon, cut through the middle.

4 In a frying pan, heat the remaining olive oil and fry the chicken on all sides on high heat.

5 Rub the chicken with the remaining tarragon and garlic. Sprinkle with salt and pepper.

6 Sprinkle with the juice of the other lemon and place in the oven.

7 Roast the chicken at 200° C (400° F or gas mark 6) for roughly 1 hour. Turn breast-side down and roast for another 30 minutes to 1 hour at 150° C (300° F or gas mark 2). Baste the chicken with the cooking juices every 15 minutes or so.

Strawberry flan

500 g (17.5 oz) strawberries,
in quarts
4 sheets puff pastry
coarse-grain sugar

For the filling:
200 g (7 oz) whipping cream
25 g (0.9 oz) sugar

1. Preheat the oven to 200 °C (400° F or gas mark 6). Press the sheets of puff pastry together with a little water and roll it out slightly.
   Cut a round out of it the size of a flan mould to make the base.
2. Brush a little water over it and sprinkle with the sugar. Bake the base for 20-25 minutes.
3. Whip the cream together with the sugar and spread this over the base.
4. Cover the crust with the strawberries.

Yoghurt with fruit and chocolate

4 tbsp sugar
1 tbsp lemon juice
100 ml (3.5 oz) water
150 ml (5.25 oz) whipping cream
400 ml (14 oz) yoghurt
150 g (5.25 oz) fresh fruit,
cut into chunks
50 g (1.75 oz) cruesli (or granola)
50 g (1.75 oz) chocolate, grated

1 Combine the sugar, lemon
  juice and water and bring
  this to the boil. Cook for
  5 minutes, then remove from
  the heat and allow to cool.
2 Whip the cream until semi-
  stiff together with the lemon-
  sugar solution and mix with
  the yoghurt.
3 Serve the mixture with fresh
  fruit, cruesli (or granola) and
  the grated chocolate.

for 20 brownies
200 g (7 oz) bittersweet
chocolate, crumbled
100 g (3.5 oz) butter
3 eggs
pinch of salt
75 g (2.5 oz) sugar
100 g (3.5 oz) brown
castor sugar
2 packets vanilla sugar
150 g (5.25 oz) self-raising
flour
100 g (3.5 oz) walnuts,
coarsely chopped
butter for greasing
20 walnut halves

Chocolate brownies with walnuts

Tip: serve with strawberries, raspberries or mixed berries, a scoop of vanilla ice cream and a dollop of whipped cream and your festive dessert is ready.

1 Melt the chocolate and butter in a bain-marie or double boiler.
2 Beat the eggs with the salt, sugar, castor sugar and vanilla sugar until foamy. Whisk in the warm chocolate mixture.
3 Add the flour and chopped walnuts and fold into the mixture.
4 Grease a 30cm x 20 cm (12" x 8") baking tin (pan) and fill with the mixture. Imagine the mixture divided into 20 pieces and place a walnut half where each of these pieces would be.
5 Bake the brownies at 175° C (335° F or gas mark 3) for 35 minutes. Remove from the oven and set aside to cool. When completely cool, remove from the pan. Cut into 20 pieces as marked by the walnut halves.

Vanilla ice cream with toffee and marshmallows

1 quart vanilla ice cream
150 g (5.25 oz) soft toffee
200 g (7 oz)
marshmallows

Tip: Children love it!

1 Place the ice cream in the refrigerator for 2 hours to let it soften.

2 Meanwhile, cut 100 g (3.5 oz) of the toffee and 100 g (3.5 oz) of the marshmallows into small pieces and mix these into the softened ice cream. Return the ice cream to the freezer to harden again.

3 Serve with the remaining toffee and marshmallows.

Strawberry mousse tartlet

1 pint strawberries, 150 g (5.25 oz) whole,
the rest in pieces
0.5 dl (1.75 oz) quark
1 egg yolk
20 g (0.7 oz) confectioner's sugar
3 egg whites
60 g (2 oz) sugar
juice of ½ lemon
3 sheets of gelatin, soaked in cold water
1 dl (3.5 oz) whipping cream, beaten until stiff
1 package brick pastry (feuille de brick)
confectioner's sugar
2 dl balsamic vinegar

Tip: You can substitute the brick pastry for filo pastry. The important thing is that the pastry is in very thin sheets.

1 Puree 150 g (5.25 oz) of the strawberries in a food processor or with a hand-held blender. Measure out 1 dl (3.5 oz) and mix this into the quark.
2 Whisk the egg yolks with the confectioner's sugar until light and airy.
3 Beat the egg whites until very stiff, whisking in the sugar bit by bit.
4 Heat the lemon juice. Drain the gelatin and dissolve it in the lemon juice.
5 Combine the beaten egg yolk with the quark.
6 Stir in the lemon juice, fold in the egg whites, then the whipped cream. Let the mousse stiffen for 4 hours.
7 Cut or press 16 rounds out of the brick pastry. Preheat the oven to 200° C (400° F or gas mark 6).
8 Cook the slices of pastry on a grill for about 15 minutes or until brown and crisp. Sprinkle with confectioner's sugar.
9 Place a slice of pastry (dough) on each of 4 plates. Spread with a generous layer of strawberry mousse, put strawberry pieces on top of this, then more dough, more mousse and more strawberries, finishing with one more slice of pastry (dough). Dust with plenty of confectioner's sugar.
10 Boil the balsamic vinegar down to half (it should be somewhat syrupy) and pour this round the tartlets.

And then there's...

A specialty coffee is the perfect thing to round off a hearty lunch. You can make Irish coffee, or hot coffee with some kind of spirits, but the best thing for a hot summer's day is iced coffee! Fill a freezer tray with cold coffee to make coffee ice cubes. Fill a glass with these and top off with more strong, sweet coffee and a dollop of whipped cream. Or pour cold coffee over scoops of vanilla, chocolate or nut ice cream. A delicious 'café frappé' can be made by freezing sweetened coffee, then crushing this in the food processor or blender. A generous dollop of whipped cream goes well with this too...

Sweet things

A splendid accompaniment for the coffee: a big bowl full of delightful sweets. For after lunch, say, or just for that mid-day coffee break, or after dinner, or at the end of the evening... You can make delicious bonbons by dipping strawberries, grapes and pieces of candied orange peel in melted (bittersweet) chocolate and letting this harden. Or chocolate-peppermint bars: mix 150 grams (5.25 oz) of chopped peppermints and the zest (grated rind) of half an orange into 200 grams (7 oz) of melted chocolate and form this mixture into a rectangle on a piece of baking paper. Once the chocolate has hardened, simply cut it into narrow strips. Also consider serving some tasty biscuits, such as the mandarin almond cookies on p. 41. And top off the bowl with chunks of nougat and caramel, Turkish delight and dried fruits such as dates and figs.

Orange cake

Orange cake

1 Preheat the oven to 180 °C (350° F or gas mark 4).

2 While the oven heats, make the cake batter. Cut the butter into small pieces using two knives.

3 Combine the butter and the flour. This is easiest if you use your fingers.

4 Add the egg yolks, the sugar and the salt and mix until you have a light and supple dough.

5 Grease a cake tin (pan) 26cm or 28 cm (10" or 11") in diameter with butter. Fill this with the batter and set aside.

6 For the filling, put the melted butter, the beaten eggs, the orange juice and the sugar in a mixing bowl.

8 Place this mixture in a double-boiler at just below boiling point, whisking immediately. Whisk constantly until the mixture begins to thicken. Be patient, because this can take some time (5 to 10 minutes). Do not try speeding up the process by turning up the heat. It simply takes time.

9 Pour the filling over the dough in the cake tin (pan).

10 Bake the cake in the preheated oven for about 25 minutes. Towards the end, prick the cake with a toothpick now and then to see if it's done. The cake is done when the toothpick comes out clean.

11 Remove from the oven and set aside to cool.

12 For the garnish, wash the oranges well and cut them into thin (2 mm) slices.

13 Put the orange slices in a saucepan together with the water and sugar and boil until soft. Make sure they don't get overdone, otherwise they become difficult to work with.

14 To make the syrup, heat the orange juice with the sugar.

15 Arrange the orange slices on top of the cake so that they completely cover it.

16 Pour the warm syrup evenly over the top.

17 Allow to cool and serve.

For the cake:
100 g (3.5 oz) butter
250 g (1 cup) flour
2 egg yolks
50 g (1.75 oz) sugar
pinch of salt

For the filling:
60 g butter, melted
5 eggs, beaten
juice of 3 oranges
200 g (7 oz) sugar

For the garnish:
2 oranges
75 g (2.5 oz) sugar
250 ml (1 cup) water

For the syrup:
2 tbsp orange juice
60 g (2 oz) sugar

menus

Menu 1

Vegetarian summer lunch

cold courgette and cumin soup (p. 66)

***

fettuccine with sage and chèvre (p. 67)

***

Provençal tartlet with sweet pepper sauce (p. 73)

salad (of your choice)

***

strawberry flan (p. 76)

Preparation

For the grocery shopping, see the ingredients list accompanying the recipes (p. 66, 67). You will also need: mixed greens and a vinaigrette of your choice. Serve a Soave or Pinot Blanc with the pasta, a full-bodied red wine from Italy or the South of France with the vegetable tartlet and a sweet sparkling wine like the Italian Asti Spumante with the strawberry flan. **One day before:** Make the soup (use vegetable stock instead of chicken stock), sweet pepper sauce and vinegar and keep it cold. Make the base for the flan. Put the white wine in the refrigerator to chill.

The day of

Finish the strawberry flan. Put the tartlets together and get them ready to go into the oven. Fry the sage leaves and sprinkle them with salt, then grate the cheese. **One hour before:** Make the salad, but do not dress it. Make the fettuccine at the last moment. Once the pasta is done, place the vegetable tartlets in the oven (preheated in good time).

3x faster

Delegate: have someone else grate the cheese, rinse and chop the lettuce and wash and slice the strawberries. **Simplify:** Buy the flan base ready-made at the bakery or supermarket (grocery store). **Leave out:** Leave the salad out, leave out the pasta dish and instead serve (fried) potatoes with the vegetable tartlet.

Menu 2

Full Easter lunch

avocado salad with oranges and cashews (p. 58)

***

red bream with crispy bacon and sereh sauce (p. 68)

***

rack of lamb on garlic-mashed potatoes with vegetables (p. 72)

***

strawberry mousse tartlet (p. 80)

Preparation

For the grocery shopping, see the ingredients list accompanying the recipes (p. 58, 68, 72, 80). Serve refreshing, light-bodied white wines with the starters: Chenin Blanc often has a hint of citrus, making it a suitable accompaniment to the salad with oranges; Sauvignon Blanc goes quite well with the cod. For the lamb, try a rich and elegant Pinot Noir from the Bourgogne. If you want to have a dessert wine as well, then go for something fruity.

One day before: Make the sereh sauce, the dressing for the salad, the strawberry mousse and the balsamic reduction. Roast the garlic to serve with the lamb. Bake the rounds of dough for the dessert and keep them in an air-tight container. Roll the red bream and basil up in the bacon. Peel the potatoes and keep them in water to prevent browning. Prepare the tomato and courgette to go into the oven and keep them covered in the refrigerator.

The day of

Peel and cut the ingredients for the salad. Coat the avocado with a bit of dressing to keep it looking fresh. Make the mashed potatoes and either keep them hot or heat them up at the last minute. One hour before: Prepare the ingredients for each dish. You can do the rest in the order in which it's to be served (don't forget that the red bream takes fifteen minutes to cook).

3x faster

Delegate: have someone else peel the potatoes, cut the tomato and courgette, peel and slice the avocado, clean the oranges...
Simplify: Buy ready-made, good-quality waffles for the mousse. Leave out: Leave out the waffles and serve the mousse with syrup in a small dish.

Menu 3

Outdoors lunch

for a lot of people, and their children

shellfish and vegetable soup (p. 64)
focaccia with cheese and dried tomato (p. 61)
***
free-range chicken with lemon and tarragon (p. 75)
stir-fried spring vegetables (p. 60)
French fries
***
chocolate brownies with walnuts (p. 78)

Preparation

An ideal lunch for a lot of people, because almost all of it can be prepared in advance. For the grocery shopping, see the ingredients list accompanying the recipes (p. 64, 61, 75, 60, 78), don't forget the French fries. For the main course, serve a South African Droë Steen or simply Steen, as the Chenin Blanc grape is called there. Have a look at p. 50-51 for tasty fruit juice ideas. **One day before:** Make the soup, the brownies and the focaccia.

The day of

Clean and cut all the vegetables. Prepare the chicken and place it in the oven to roast. **One hour before:** Everything is at the ready, the only thing that needs to be done at the last minute is the stir-fry: this should take 5 to 10 minutes.

3x faster

Delegate: Have someone else cut the vegetables or cook the French fries. **Simplify:** In the morning, briefly cook the vegetables in a wok, let them cool, then place them in a baking dish. Put this in the oven when the chicken has about 10 minutes to go. Buy pre-baked focaccia and heat it at the last moment. **Leave out:** You can also leave the focaccia out altogether.

Carpaccio

Salmon carpaccio, tuna carpaccio, aubergine or beetroot carpaccio, even melon or apple carpaccio...! Purists, of course, will tell you that it's only true carpaccio if it's made from tenderloin. But the name rolls off your tongue so nicely, and the paper-thin slices are an especially attractive way to present your creation!

And this is to say nothing of the greatest advantage of carpaccio, namely that for most meals you can plate this dish up a few hours in advance, then simply drizzle a little dressing over it right before serving (this can be made a day in advance as well). Garnish the plate here and there with a lettuce leaf, and your stress-free starter is ready. And also, just about everyone is perfectly happy with this dish, whether you let your imagination run wild or stick to the most traditional kind!

The one and only

The original carpaccio, by the way, is not the one with the pine nuts, Parmesan cheese and olive oil, as is commonly believed. The inventor of the carpaccio, Giuseppe Cipriani of Harry's Bar in Venice (where the Bellini cocktail was also invented, in case you were wondering) made this dish with a creamy sauce of mayonnaise, mustard and Worcestershire sauce. Cipriani named the dish after Vittore Carpaccio, the Italian renaissance painter – because the bright red of the tenderloin and the creamy white of the sauce made him think of Carpaccio's paintings.

Concentration

Making carpaccio at home is not difficult, though cutting it does take some concentration – and patience. You can save yourself a lot of trouble by having the butcher do it for you! If you do choose to cut it yourself, put the meat in the freezer for 20 minutes before you cut it, as this makes it easier to get those thin slices. This also works for fish. Go for firm fish varieties, like tuna. It goes without saying that you need a very sharp knife for this. A trick for beginners: cut somewhat thicker slices, place these between two sheets of plastic wrap and pound them flat with a frying pan or rolling pin. Just like the real thing!

Herbed melon

1 melon, thinly sliced – 100 g (3.5 oz) watercress **For the herb dressing:** 2 tbsp basil – 1 tbsp mint – 2 tbsp balsamic vinegar – 1 tbsp honey – tsp coarse mustard – 2 tbsp maize-germ oil – 2 tbsp olive oil

1 Blend the ingredients for the dressing with a hand-held blender and season with salt and pepper to taste.
2 Divide the melon over 4 plates. Drizzle with the dressing
3 Garnish with sprigs of watercress.

Tuna with tomato tapenade

200 g (7 oz) fresh tuna– 4 sprigs watercress
For the tomato tapenade:
250 g (1 cup) green olives, pitted – 1 clove of garlic, very finely chopped– 1 tbsp cognac – 1 tsp lemon juice – 6 sun-dried tomatoes, finely chopped – 2 tbsp Parmesan cheese, grated – 50 ml (1.75 oz) olive oil

1 Roll the tuna up in plastic film (wrap) and keep it in the freezer for 4 hours.
2 Put all the ingredients in a food processor and blend them to a chunky paste. If desired, add salt and pepper to taste.
3 Cut the tuna into very thin slices and arrange them over 4 plates.
4 Spread 4 tablespoons of the tapenade over the middle and garnish with the watercress.
5 Sprinkle with a little salt and freshly ground pepper.

Beetroot with herring salad

4 large red beets, boiled – 5 tbsp white wine vinegar –
1 tbsp coarse mustard – 2 tbsp olive oil – 2 tbsp maize-
germ oil – 1 tsp sugar – 1 tsp honey – 2 herrings, cut into
small pieces – 1 green onion, in rings – 1 onion, very finely
chopped

1 Make the marinade: combine the vinegar, mustard, oil,
   sugar and honey and mix well.
2 Cut the beets into thin, even slices. Cover with the
   marinade and allow to sit for around 4 hours (turning
   regularly).
3 Put the beets in a strainer or colander to drain (keep the
   marinade for later) and place one each on 4 plates.
4 Combine the herrings with the chopped onion and a little
   marinade and mound this right on top of the beets. Pour
   the remaining marinade over top.

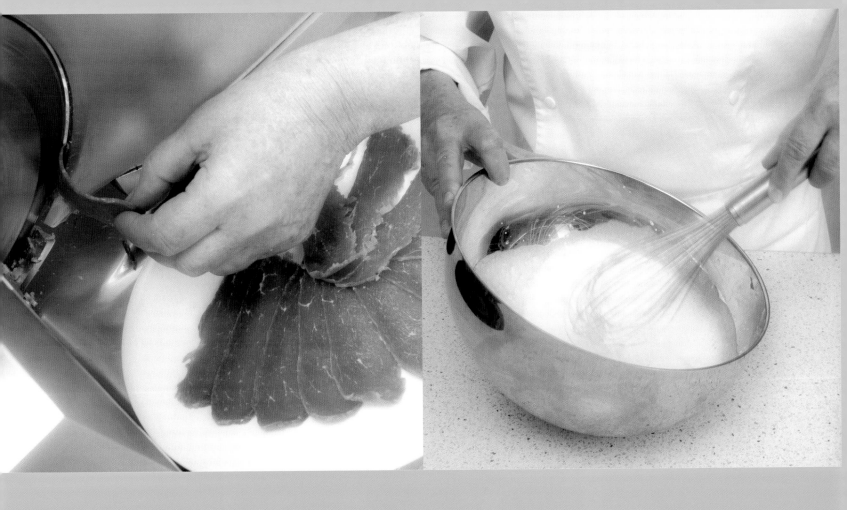

Carpaccio alla Giuseppe

400 g (14 oz) tenderloin– 60 ml (2 oz) mayonnaise (preferably home-made) – 2 to 3 tbsp whipping cream – 2 tsp Worcestershire sauce – 2 tsp mild mustard – Tabasco – rocket

1 Cut the tenderloin into paper-thin slices.
2 Combine the mayonnaise, whipping cream, Worcestershire sauce and mustard and stir to a thick sauce. Season with Tabasco and a pinch of salt to taste.
3 Divide the tenderloin over 4 plates.
4 Drizzle with the sauce and serve with rocket and freshly grated pepper.

BBQ

Back garden fiesta

The air above the grill sizzles from the red coals, the garden is at is best and the table is set in bright and festive colours. Bowls of flowers and whole pineapples and mangos provide a tropical atmosphere, no matter what you have growing in the garden. The drinks will stay quite cold if you put them in a metal tub or other container full of ice – bottles of Caribbean beers, blush wines and maybe a bottle of tequila or rum for the cocktails. If you have a brazier, this should be all filled and ready for when dusk falls and a chill sets in. And don't forget the hot coffee (with a dash of rum for some) and sweet and sticky almond cookies. Isn't it great to spend the whole evening outside?

There's no better group for a barbecue than your own best friends. Barbecuing can be a lot of fun with everybody outside and helping out, or just patiently waiting until the next course is ready to be served. What you need then is simply any group of people who enjoy each other's company. And, thanks to these tasty recipes, you will have plenty to talk about... and plenty of good times to think back on!

Imaginative

The second most important thing? The food. The days when barbecuing was a synonym for heaps of cheap meat are fortunately over. Nowadays there are the most sumptuous barbecue recipes from all over the world. Pick them with care: two or three imaginative dishes certainly make a bigger impression than six different kinds of ready-made marinated meat! And there's nowhere it says you can't put fish on the grill either: tilapia is great barbecued inside a banana leaf. It stays wonderfully moist and develops an exotic flavour from the banana leaves. Or make spicy prawns, which just about everybody loves. And even if there's a vegetarian (or several) in your party, fruit and veggies on the grill can be fantastic. Try aubergines with goat's cheese, or button mushrooms marinated in a spicy sauce...

From March to November

And don't worry about the weather too much. It doesn't have to be exactly summertime temperatures (unless perhaps you want to give the party a tropical theme... in that case, save it for August). If it's perfectly normal to barbecue in the middle of winter in Canada and Scandinavia (and it certainly is), then surely the rest of us should be able to hold out from March to November, right? For extra certainty, you can always stretch out a tarp, put up an awning or set up a party tent; the important thing is to not let gloomy weather forecasts hold you back from enjoying yourself. If it's cold, just put on a sweater, or you can all go sit closer to the fire. Nice and snug...

Sangria

Still one of the tastiest summer drinks! Into a large carafe pour two bottles of red wine, three tablespoons of fine-grain sugar, 10 ml (0.35 oz) orange liqueur and 2 oranges, 2 lemons and 2 limes, all in slices. Let the wine sit overnight, when ready to serve, top off with plenty of ice and a half bottle of sparkling mineral water.

Pyromaniacs

There are most likely a few people in your circle of friends who are all too eager to get the fire going on their own. Everybody has his or her own strategy for doing so. Whatever the case, make sure that the grill is lit on time, because the process takes a while. It won't be ready to grill for about half an hour, or until the flames have all died down and the coals are covered in a thin haze of light. This is when it's at its best. Try to arrange the coals so you have one portion hot and the other somewhat less, because some dishes require more heat than others. Make sure you replenish with new coals well in advance of the next course, otherwise you might end up without a fire.

Beefsteak roll-ups

8 x 60 g (2 oz) slices of beefsteak
1 sweet red pepper
4 anchovies, chopped
4 black olives, chopped
1 tbsp capers
freshly grated pepper

For the dressing:
4 tbsp olive oil
3 tbsp balsamic vinegar

1 Roast the pepper at 220° C (425° F or gas mark 7) in a pre-heated oven for 35 minutes, or until blackened.
2 Remove from the oven, cover and allow to cool for 20 minutes, then remove the peel and core.
3 Finely dice the pepper and mix this with the anchovy, capers and olives.
4 Tenderise the beef and top with the diced pepper.
5 Roll the slices up and stick a toothpick through each to keep it closed.
6 Fry the roll-ups on each side in 1 tablespoon of olive oil for about 3 minutes.
7 Mix 3 tablespoon of olive oil and 3 tablespoons of balsamic vinegar. Warm the dressing slightly.
8 Serve 2 roll-ups per person on a lukewarm plate.
9 Drizzle with the olive oil dressing and freshly grated pepper.

Artichoke bottoms with crayfish and sherry mayonnaise

For 8 people
8 large artichokes
250 g (8.75 oz) crayfish tails, boiled
juice of 1 lemon
250 g (8.75 oz) broccoli, in florets, blanched and cooled
2 green onions, sliced into thin rings
lemon slices
salt and freshly ground pepper

For the mayonnaise:
1 egg yolk
1 tsp Dijon mustard
2 tbsp sherry vinegar
1 tbsp sherry
2 dl (7 oz) maize-germ oil
pinch of salt

1 Halve each artichoke through the middle, just above the heart. Using a spoon, remove the hairs. With a potato peeler, remove the remaining leaves from the artichoke bottom.

2 Boil the artichoke bottoms in water, lemon juice and sugar for roughly 20 minutes, or until tender.

3 For the mayonnaise, combine the egg yolk, Dijon mustard, vinegar, sherry and salt in a narrow measuring jug (pint-size). Pour in the oil and position a hand-held blender so that the blades are at the very bottom of the jug. Start the blender and slowly raise it as soon as the mayonnaise at the bottom of the cup thickens.

4 Toss the broccoli, crayfish tails and spring onion with the mayonnaise and salt to taste.

5 Fill the artichoke bottoms with the mayonnaise and serve with a lemon slice and freshly grated pepper.

Herbed lamb and aubergine kabobs

12 skewers
400 g (14 oz) tender lamb, cubed
1 tbsp ground coriander
1 tsp ground cumin
2 cloves of garlic, chopped
1 tsp ground black pepper
1 tsp sea salt
4 tbsp olive oil
1 dl (3.5 oz) yoghurt
12 strips (lengthwise slices) of aubergine
salt

1 Marinate the meat for roughly 1 hour with the coriander, cumin, garlic, salt, pepper, 2 tbsp olive oil and yoghurt.
2 Salt the aubergine strips and place in a colander for 1 hour for the bitter liquid to drain.
3 Pat the aubergine dry with a paper towel and coat with 2 tablespoons olive oil
4 Fill 12 skewers with the meat and aubergine.
5 Fry these in a hot dry pan or above the fire.

For 8 people

800 g (28 oz) boneless chicken legs
1½ tsp ground allspice
½ tsp ground cinnamon
1 onion, cut into chunks
4 cloves of garlic
2 red chili peppers, seeded
1 tbsp thyme
2 cm (0.8") ginger root, peeled
2 tbsp soy sauce
2 tbsp lemon juice
1 ½ tsp salt

Tip: 'Jerk' is originally a Jamaican dish made from pieces of meat, chicken or fish, which are then fried or roasted. You can also use this marinade for tender pieces of beef or any firm fish. Serve with hot salsa.

Jerk chicken

1 In a food processor, blend all the ingredients (except the chicken) to a smooth sauce.
2 Cut the chicken into cubes and place in a mixing bowl. Cover the meat with the sauce and place in the refrigerator for 8 hours to marinate.
3 Thread the cubes of chicken onto a skewer and bake in a pre-heated oven at 180° C (350° F or gas mark 4) for 10 minutes or until cooked through. (Otherwise you run the risk of the chicken not getting done on the grill alone.)
4 Finish the skewers off on the barbecue.

Spicy prawns

400 g (14 oz) raw prawns, cleaned
1 clove of garlic, chopped
2 red chili peppers, seeded and minced
100 ml (3.5 oz) olive oil

1 Combine all the ingredients and allow to sit for at least 6 hours to marinate.
2 Broil the prawns with the oil in a heat-resistant dish. Serve immediately, with bread or salad on the side.

Tip: Only turn the kebabs once to keep the fish from falling apart.

For 8 people
For the kebab:
400 g (14 oz) firm fish fillets (Nile perch, seawolf, angler or monkfish, etc.), in 16 pieces
1 tsp curry powder
16 king prawns
1 sweet red pepper, cut into 8 pieces
8 cherry tomatoes
2 red onions, quartered
4 tbsp oil
salt and pepper

For the salsa:
200 g (7 oz) watermelon, cut into small cubes
100 g (3.5 oz) cucumber, deseeded and cut into small cubes
1 red chili pepper, deseeded and sliced into thin strips
zest (grated rind) of ½ a lime
juice of 1 lime
salt and pepper

Fish kebab with melon salsa

1 Rub the pieces of fish with the curry powder.
2 Slide the pieces of fish, prawns, sweet pepper, tomato and onion onto wooden skewers (these should first be soaked in water). Coat with oil and sprinkle with salt and pepper.
3 Combine all the ingredients for the salsa and season with salt and pepper to taste.
4 Grill the skewers for about 3 minutes on each side. Serve with the salsa.

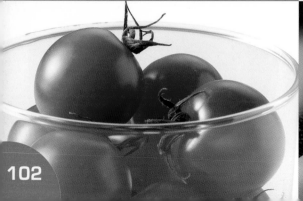

Red bream with rosemary

4 small red bream, gutted
4 sprigs of rosemary
2 tbsp olive oil
1 tbsp chili oil
juice of 1 lemon
salt and pepper

1 Stuff the fish with rosemary and coat with the oil, salt and pepper.
2 Barbecue the fish over moderate heat and drizzle with lemon juice.

Bread salad

4 pitas
1 cucumber, diced
3 tomatoes, deseeded and diced
1 green onion, sliced
1 red onion, cut into ringlets
1 tbsp mint leaves, chopped
2 tbsp fresh coriander (cilantro), chopped
2 cloves of garlic, chopped
6 tbsp olive oil
juice of 1 lemon
salt and pepper

1 For the dressing, combine the olive oil, lemon juice, salt and pepper.
2 Mix the pieces of cucumber, tomato and green onion with the dressing.
3 Broil the bread until crispy, then crumble it into small pieces.
4 Toss the pieces of bread with all the other ingredients and season with salt and pepper to taste.

Rice salad

200 g (7 oz) wild rice, boiled
100 g (3.5 oz) almonds
juice of 1 orange
4 tbsp olive oil
1 tsp lemon zest
100 g (3.5 oz) rocket leaves
50 g (1.75 oz) raisins
salt and pepper

1 Toast the almonds.
2 Combine the orange juice with the olive oil and lemon zest and season with salt and pepper to taste.
3 Toss all the ingredients together and serve in a salad bowl.

400 g (14 oz) tilapia fillets,
in 8 pieces
8 banana leaves
2 tbsp lime juice
2 cm (0.8") ginger root,
grated
1 tbsp honey

For the marinade:
2 cloves of garlic, minced
1 tsp black pepper,
ground
1 tbsp ginger syrup
1 stalk of lemongrass
75 ml (2.5 oz),
light soy sauce
1 tbsp Worcestershire
sauce

Banana leaf tilapia

1 For the marinade, puree all the ingredients in a food processor.
   Place the fish in the sauce and marinate for at least 2, but preferably
   8 hours.
2 Blanch the banana leaves for a few minutes in boiling water.
3 Remove the pieces of fish from the marinade and pat dry. Combine the
   lime juice, ginger and honey and coat the fish with this mixture.
   Wrap the fish in banana leaves and stick a toothpick through each one
   to keep it closed.
4 Grill the fish parcels on the barbecue.

Tip: Banana leaves can usually
be found in Asian import shops.
If there are none available, then
simply use aluminium foil for
wrapping the fish.

Caribbean ribs with mango sauce

For 8 people

1.6 kg (3.5 lbs) lamb ribs
1 tbsp curry powder
1 tsp ground cumin
1 tsp cayenne pepper
2 dl (7 oz) soy sauce
100 g (3.5 oz) brown
sugar
juice of 1 lime

For the sauce:

2 tbsp brown sugar
juice of 1 lime
2 tbsp Thai fish sauce
2 mangos,
peeled and diced
2 cm (0.8 ") ginger root,
peeled and very
finely chopped
½ sweet red pepper,
diced
1 tbsp chives
1 tbsp fresh coriander
(cilantro), chopped

1 Heat the curry powder, cumin and cayenne pepper in a dry pan for one minute.
2 Pour in the soy sauce, followed by the sugar. Stir well until the sugar has completely dissolved. Pour the sauce out of the pan into another container and mix in the lemon juice.
3 Marinate the ribs for 8 hours in the sauce, turning occasionally.
4 For the sauce, dissolve the sugar in the lemon juice and fish sauce. Mix all the remaining ingredients into this sauce.
5 Barbecue the ribs until crispy. Serve with the sauce.

Tip: Halve some limes and place them cut-side down on the barbecue grill until they develop dark grill marks. Squeeze the grilled limes over the ribs for a refreshing accent. Delicious with all sorts of grilled fish as well.

Prawn skewers with ham

20 prawns, peeled – 20 basil leaves – 10 slices raw ham

For the marinade: 2 tbsp olive oil – 2 tbsp lemon juice – 1 sprig of thyme, leaves only – 1 clove of garlic, pressed

For the herb sauce: – 1 tbsp parsley – 1 tbsp oregano – 2 cloves of garlic, pressed – rind of 2 lemons, in strips – juice of 2 lemons – 1 red chili pepper, stemmed, seeded and very finely chopped

1 Combine all the ingredients for the marinade and let the prawns sit in this mixture for 10 minutes.

2 Wrap the prawns in some basil and a slice of raw ham. Slide them onto skewers.

3 Combine the ingredients for the herb sauce.

4 Grill the skewers for 10 minutes on the barbecue, or until brown, and serve with the herb sauce.

Sardines in grape leaves

12 large grape leaves
12 sardines
2 tbsp parsley, chopped
2 tbsp coriander (cilantro), chopped
3 cloves of garlic, chopped
3 tbsp olive oil
juice of 1 lemon
salt and pepper

1 Remove the heads and tails from the sardines.
2 Place the fish flat and slice open the belly. Remove the innards and spine.
3 Rinse the sardines with water.
4 Make a herb mixture of olive oil, parsley, coriander, salt and pepper.
5 Stuff the sardines with the herb mixture and wrap them in the grape leaves.
6 Broil the fish in the oven or on the barbecue. Sprinkle with lemon juice and serve.

Tip: Instead of sardines you can also use fresh mackerel.

On turning meat

Some people have the tendency to continually turn meat as it cooks. This is really not the best thing for it. It's better to wait until a crust has formed, then gently ease it from the grill. If the meat is charred on both sides, move it to another part of the grill which is not quite as hot so that it can continue cooking without burning. Some types of meat, such as steaks, do not need to cook all the way through, of course. There is an interesting trick to determine how done a steak is: gently hold the thumb and index finger of one hand together. With the finger of your other hand, feel the area just below the thumb. This is how a 'rare' steak feels when you press on it. Now hold the thumb and middle finger together and feel the same part: this is how 'medium rare' should feel. Thumb to ring finger is 'medium' and thumb to pinky is 'well done'. (Okay, it's not exactly scientific, but it gives you a pretty good idea.)

Tofu and tempé saté

The Caribbean comes to you

For a summer party, set up some torches in your back garden and decorate the table in Caribbean style with natural materials and clear, bright colours. This will give it a really festive, tropical atmosphere. For each place setting put a serviette of a different colour, nicely rolled up and tied with a piece of raffia. You can also place a nice flower in between. Use banana leaves (available at many Asian import shops) as a natural plate for smaller snacks. Palm leaves (try the florist) also make great place mats. And don't forget the rum! Try a mixed drink, like the fruity rum punch from chapter 4.

Tip: Soak wooden skewers in cold water for fifteen minutes before use, this will prevent them from burning on the grill.

½ block tofu, in cubes
½ block tempé, in cubes
2 cloves of garlic, very finely chopped
2 tbsp lemon juice
2 tbsp Indonesian ketjap manis
1 shallot, very finely chopped
1 tbsp olive oil
1 red chili pepper, very finely chopped
2 tbsp soy sauce

1 For the marinade, combine garlic, lemon juice and ketjap manis.
2 Marinate the tofu in this mixture for 30 minutes.
3 Heat the olive oil and sauté the shallot and red chili for 3 minutes. Add the soy sauce and stir well.
4 Marinate the tempé in this mixture for 30 minutes.
5 Slide the tofu and the tempé onto skewers, alternating the pieces. Make sure the skewer does not stick out at the top.
6 Grill the saté skewers for 5 minutes on the barbecue, turning regularly.

Aubergine parcels with goat's cheese

2 aubergines, cut into long thin slices
200 g (7 oz) soft goat's cheese
2 tbsp olive oil
2 shallots, very finely chopped
1 clove of garlic, pressed
50 g (1.75 oz) black olives, finely chopped
50 g (1.75 oz) almonds, chopped
salt and pepper

1   Grill the aubergine slices on the barbecue.
2   Heat the olive oil and sauté the shallots and garlic until translucent.
3   Add the olives and almonds and cook for another 2 minutes.
4   Season with salt and pepper to taste and take off the heat to cool.
5   Spread the goat's cheese over the aubergine slices and roll them up.
6   Top with the shallot mixture.

Tip: The aubergine slices must be paper thin, otherwise it will be difficult to fold them into parcels and they will not cook through properly.

Grilled vegetable salad

3 sweet Turkish (long) peppers
5 thin Turkish eggplants
5 tomatoes
6 tbsp lemon juice
12 tbsp olive oil
1 tbsp fresh mint leaves, chopped
2 cloves of garlic, very finely chopped
½ bunch parsley, finely chopped

1 Slide the vegetables onto saté skewers and place them direct on the coals, so that the peels blacken: first the sweet peppers, then after a few minutes the aubergines and finally the tomatoes.

2 Let the vegetables cool off a bit, then pull off the peels (it's okay if there are still a few pieces sticking to them).

3 Dice the cooked vegetables, then make a dressing of lemon juice, olive oil, mint, garlic, parsley, salt and pepper and toss with the remaining ingredients.

4 Serve room temperature.

8 brown button mushrooms
8 spring onions
8 tbsp spicy marinade

For the marinade:
2 tbsp sesame oil
2 tbsp Japanese sukiyaki sauce
1 cm (0.4") ginger root, chopped
1 tbsp honey
1 tbsp lemon juice

Tip: This is a delicious marinade for other vegetables as well, though the advantage of mushrooms is that they really absorb the flavour of the marinade. Aubergines have the same trait. Combine either one of these with some other vegetables for optimal flavour.

Mushrooms and spring onions

1 Mix all the ingredients for the marinade in a blender.
2 Cut the green onion into pieces of approx. 7 cm (2.75").
3 Remove the stalks from the mushrooms.
4 Slide the green onion and mushrooms onto skewers and let these sit for 1 hour in the marinade.
5 Grill the skewers on the barbecue and serve immediately.

Wines, defined

Finding the right wine to go with your barbecue can be a difficult task. There is often a variety of dishes to choose from, several meats as well as fish, and everybody wants something different. Adding to the confusion, there is rarely a clear distinction between what's the starter, main course and side dish. Not to mention the fact that barbecue dishes are often quite potently seasoned, with a very pronounced smoky flavour. The delicate bouquet of fine wines is easily overwhelmed – meaning it's probably best not to break out that special bottle you've been saving. Instead, go for a pure and simple table wine. South African wines are often wonderfully rich in flavour and very well suited for a proper braai, the Afrikaans word for BBQ. Other suitable red wines are the Cabernet Sauvignons from 'new' wine countries like Chile, Argentina or Australia, owing to their soft and well-rounded flavour. An ordinary blush wine is also a safe bet, and not at all out of place with, say, a charburger. Try a Côtes de Provence, which goes really well with a whole array of dishes. If you're a fan of white wines, then pick one made from a full-flavoured grape variety like Chardonnay or Pinot Grigio. You can try a different approach too. Instead of letting everyone grill their own, turn the barbecue into a multi-course meal, deciding on your own when to serve which dish. This will allow the guests to take it easy and wait patiently (or not!) for the next course. It also means that you can be more specific about which wines to combine with which courses. (Also have a look at the menu suggestions on p. 123-125)

Herb ricotta-stuffed potatoes

For 8 people:

8 large potatoes, leave jackets on

4 tbsp olive oil

8 cloves of garlic, crushed

8 sprigs of thyme

For the herb ricotta:

200 g (7 oz) ricotta

100 g (3.5 oz) crème fraîche

2 tbsp chives, chopped

2 tbsp flat-leaf parsley, chopped

1 tbsp oregano, chopped

1 clove of garlic,
very finely chopped

salt and pepper

1 Scrub the potatoes clean and brush them with 1 tbsp oil. Wrap them in aluminium foil together with a crushed clove of garlic and a sprig of thyme. Bake at 200° C (400° F or gas mark 6) for one hour.

2 Make the herb ricotta: combine all the ingredients called for and mix well. Add salt and pepper to taste.

3 Remove the cooked potatoes from the foil, slice the top off of each one and scoop out some of the inside. Fill with the herb ricotta.

Tip: It also looks quite nice if you make a cross in the top of the cooked potatoes (cut fairly deeply), then carefully push them open by squeezing with both hands in the middle of the potato. The inside of the potato will well up, creating space in the peel for more filling. Also very tasty with herb butter, tomato sauce, fried mushrooms or smoked salmon and a dollop of sour cream! If you're short on time, an easy shortcut is to pre-bake the potatoes in the microwave. First prick them with a fork and wrap each one in a paper towel. Five minutes at high heat will cut the baking time in half.

Grilled fruit

It may well be that the most delicious desserts are the ones right off the grill! Take, for example, these tasty **fruit skewers**. Some good fruits for this are pineapple, mango, strawberry, pear, peach, banana, apple, grape and melon. Marinate the skewers for a little while in a simple syrup: just combine 100 g (3.5 oz) sugar with 100 ml (3.5 oz) water and heat the solution on the stove, adding a dash of whatever liqueur you want for flavour. Grill the skewers until the fruit begins to caramelise. Or cut **whole bananas (skin and all)** in half and sprinkle the cut side with a mixture of palm sugar (or brown castor sugar) and grated coconut. Place them on the barbecue peel-side down and grill until the sugar melts. Serve with a scoop of (coconut) ice cream.

Also quite delectable are **foil parcels filled** with fruit, such as berries and peach halves. Add a generous dollop of rum butter: whisk two tablespoons brown castor sugar and four tablespoons confectioner's sugar into 100 grams (3.5 oz) of butter, then stir in two (or more!) tablespoons of rum until the rum has been completely absorbed by the butter. Dust the fruit with a little extra sugar if you like and grill the parcels for a few minutes or until the fruit has softened. The butter will mix with the fruit juice and create a brilliant sauce.

Tip: You can also use ready-made frozen pastry (dough), but be warned that the flavour is not the same. If using frozen pastry (dough), sprinkle with turmeric before rolling it out.

for approx. 16 pieces: 500 g (17.5 oz) flour – 1 tsp turmeric – ½ tsp salt – 125 g (4.5 oz) butter – 2 dl (7 oz) water

for the filling: 400 g (14 oz) minced beef – 1 onion, very finely chopped – 2 cloves garlic, very finely chopped – 1 red chili pepper, seeded and very finely chopped – 1 tsp ground cardamom – 1 tsp ground allspice – 1 tsp turmeric – 1 tsp cumin seed – 1 tsp thyme – 3 tomatoes, finely chopped – 1 egg, beaten – salt

1 Sift the flour, turmeric and salt into a mixing bowl. Cut the butter into small pieces and quickly rub this into the flour with your fingertips until it resembles fine breadcrumbs. Add water and knead the pastry (dough) into a ball. Cover tightly in plastic film (wrap) and place in the refrigerator for at least 1 hour.
2 Sauté the onion, garlic and pepper in the oil. Add the spices and the thyme and cook a few minutes longer.
3 Add the mincemeat and tomatoes. Cook until the liquid from the tomatoes has evaporated and the mincemeat is cooked through. Add salt and pepper to taste. Remove from the heat and allow to cool.
4 Roll the pastry (dough) out to a sheet about 3 mm thick. Cut out small rounds of approx. 12 cm (4.5"). Place a spoonful of filling in the centre of each round, fold closed and crimp the edges together with the prongs of a fork. Place the pasties on a greased and floured baking sheet. Brush with a beaten egg and bake at 180° C (350° F or gas mark 4) for 20 minutes or until golden brown.

Jamaican pasties

Courgette with potato salad

4 courgettes, cut into 4 slices lengthwise
1 dl (3.5 oz) olive oil
3 cloves of garlic, chopped
1 red chili pepper, cut into strips
1 dl (3.5 oz) red wine vinegar
1 bunch of fresh basil
sea salt

For the potato salad:
6 potatoes, leave jackets on
1 clove of garlic, chopped
6 tbsp olive oil
1 tbsp parsley, finely chopped
1 tbsp tarragon
salt and pepper

1   Sprinkle the slices of courgette with salt and place them in a colander to drain for 30 minutes.
2   Pat dry with a paper towel.
3   Fry in the oil until golden brown and place in a dish.
4   Briefly sauté the garlic with the pepper and pour in the vinegar.
5   Add this sauce, together with the basil leaves, to the courgette slices. This dish can be served cold.
6   Brush the potatoes clean for the potato salad, boil them until cooked through, then peel.
7   Cut them into slices and arrange them in rows domino-style on a serving dish.
8   Combine the garlic, oil, salt and pepper.
9   Add the garlic oil to the potatoes and sprinkle with the herbs.

Tip: The courgettes can also be grilled, of course. They are delicious warm. If you can't find any tarragon, dill will work in a pinch. It doesn't taste the same, but also goes quite well with potatoes.

Precision work

Perhaps the most difficult part of barbecuing is getting the meat and fish just the right temperature before it goes onto the grill. Taking it directly out of the refrigerator will make it too cold, meaning the inside will be raw while the outside starts to burn. But leaving meat and fish at room temperature for too long is also not a very good idea, for obvious health reasons. The optimal thing is to let it come up to temperature in a reasonably cool room about one hour beforehand. Whatever you do, don't leave meat and fish sitting out in the hot sun! Remove it from the refrigerator in portions and take it outside at the very last minute.

The old herb brush

If you want a quick dish, instead of ready-made marinated meat, buy some good-quality meat or fish which can go right on the grill in its 'natural' state, with nothing more than some salt and pepper. To prevent it from sticking to the grill, coat it with a little (olive) oil, using a brush you can make yourself from a bundle of woody herbs tied with a piece of string (thyme and rosemary work well). This rustic little tool looks charming and lends the meat a subtle herb flavour. The barbecue will do the rest...

Pretty little bottles

Collect about ten or so empty, not overly large bottles of various heights, remove the labels and clean them well. Arrange flowers or fresh branches in them. For a really nice look, add a bit of food colouring to the water.

Guacamole

Everybody loves guacamole! Mash three ripe avocados with the following finely chopped ingredients: one shallot, one peeled tomato, one sprig of cilantro, one green chili pepper and one clove of garlic. Season with a level teaspoon of salt and the juice of one lime. You can keep guacamole from turning brown by covering the surface with a sheet of plastic wrap. This will prevent oxygen from getting to it.

Fruit soup with lemon sorbet

For 6 people
For the sorbet:
150 ml (5.25 oz) water
150 g (5.25 oz) sugar
2 tbsp lemon zest
juice of 10 lemons
For the fruit soup:
250 g (8.75 oz or 1 cup) berries
250 ml (1 cup) sweet
German wine
50 g (1.75 oz) sugar
juice of 1 lemon

1 Boil the water with the sugar and lemon zest.
2 Mix in the lemon juice to bring the total volume to 70 ml (2.5 oz).
3 Freeze the mixture in an ice cream maker.
4 For the fruit soup, boil the wine and sugar.
5 Add the fruit and lemon juice.
6 Serve the soup cold with the lemon sorbet.

Portuguese almond diamonds

100 g (3.5 oz) almonds
200 g (7 oz) softened butter
250 g (8.75 oz) confectioner's sugar
seeds of 1 vanilla bean
5 eggs, separated
1 tbsp rum
250 g (8.75 oz) flour
1 tbsp lemon juice
For the garnish:
50 g (1.75 oz) almond slivers
3 tbsp confectioner's sugar

1 Grind the almonds in a blender until fine.
2 Combine the butter, confectioner's sugar and vanilla seeds.
3 Whisk the egg yolks into the butter one at a time, then add the rum.
4 Mix in the flour in 3 steps.
5 Beat the egg whites with lemon juice until foamy but not too stiff.
6 Combine with the ground almonds, then with the batter.
7 Spread the batter out over unwaxed paper on a 25cm x 25 cm (10" x 10") baking sheet.
8 Sprinkle with almond slivers and confectioner's sugar.
9 Bake at 180° C (350° F or gas mark 4) for 50 minutes. Cut the sheet into diamond shapes. Garnish with almond slivers and sugar.

menus

Menu 1

Caribbean BBQ

Jamaican pasties (p. 117)

***

banana leaf tilapia (p. 106)

jerk chicken (p. 100)

melon salsa (p. 102)

Caribbean ribs with mango sauce (p. 107)

***

grilled fruit (p. 116)

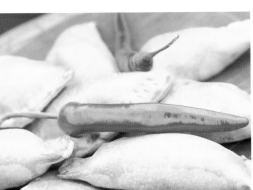  

Preparation

For the grocery shopping, see the ingredients list accompanying the recipes (p. 117, 106, 100, 102, 107, 116). You will also need ingredients for the melon salsa (see p. 102) and tropical fruit for grilling (see p. 116). For this barbecue, serve cocktails with rum, such as the fruity rum punch on p. 146, and summer fruit drinks (see p. 50). One day before: Marinate the ribs, chicken and fish. Make the mango sauce (but wait until the last minute to add the herbs). Skewer the chicken. Blanch the banana leaves. Make the filling and the pastry (dough) for the pasties, keeping them separate. Make the simple syrup for the fruit dessert.

The day of

Make the tilapia parcels. Fill the pasties and place them on a baking sheet (but do not brush with the egg yet). Clean the fruit, put it on skewers and marinate it. Make the salsa. Finish the mango sauce. **One hour before:** Light the barbecue. Finish the pasties.

3x faster

Delegate: Have someone else skewer the fruit and the meat, clean fruit, chop ingredients for salsa, light the barbecue, etc. **Simplify:** Buy ready-made salsa. Buy mango chutney instead of mango sauce and stir in fresh herbs. **Leave out:** Choose another starter than the pasties, perhaps the stuffed papayas on p. 145. Leave out one of the main dishes and make a little more of another one. Buy ready-made tropical fruit salad for dessert.

Menu 2

Elegant 6-course barbecue

artichoke bottoms with crayfish and sherry mayonnaise (p. 98)

***

red bream with rosemary (p. 103)

***

aubergine parcels with goat's cheese (p. 111)

***

beef roll-ups with pimientos (p. 97)

***

Portuguese almond diamonds (p. 121)

***

deluxe coffee (p. 81)

Preparation

For the grocery shopping, see the ingredients list accompanying the recipes (p. 98, 103, 111, 97, 121, 81). You will also need: a large bowl of salad, a basket of fresh bread and tapenade (see p. 152). For this barbecue, serve a selection of wines and cold mineral water. One day before: Bake the almond diamonds and keep them in an air-tight container. Make the beef roll-ups and prep the artichokes. Make the mayonnaise. Keep everything in the refrigerator and chill the wine and mineral water.

The day of

Prepare the aubergine and red bream. Finish the artichoke snacks. One hour before: You should have everything ready by the time your guests arrive. Offer them a cold glass of Prosecco as soon as they arrive and (once everyone is sitting down) the artichokes. Put the bread and salad on the table if the red bream is ready. Serve the dishes at a leisurely pace. (Get the barbecue going with plenty of time to spare, because the beef roll-ups require a hot fire.)

Menu 3

Mezze barbecue

pita and hummus (p. 74)
marinated olives
grilled vegetable salad (p. 113)
sardines in grape leaves (p. 109)
herbed lamb and aubergine kabobs (p. 99)
bread salad (p. 105)

***

fruit and sweets

Preparation

Mezze are Middle-Eastern tapas: a whole bunch of savoury snacks, salads and dips to try. For the grocery shopping, see the ingredients list accompanying the recipes (p. 74, 113, 109, 99, 105). You will also need: ingredients for hummus (see p. 74), extra pita or flatbread, marinated olives and, if desired, some more snacks and salads from your nearest Turkish greengrocer. Here you can also find sweets and special fruits for the dessert (see also p. 116). For this barbecue, serve raki or ouzo (a distilled anise-flavoured drink) as aperitif, followed by fruit juice or red wine: Moroccan, if you can find it, otherwise perhaps an Argentine Malbec. After the meal, it's a traditional to offer strong coffee or sweet mint tea from small glasses. **One day before:** Make the hummus. Get the sardines ready for the grill and keep them covered in the refrigerator. Marinate the lamb. Make the salad dressings.

The day of

Salt the aubergine for the skewers, wait an hour, then finish prepping the lamb skewers. Cut the vegetables and toast the pita bread for the salad. **One hour before:** Finish making the bread salad and get everything else ready for your guests. And relax!

3x faster

Delegate: Have someone else cut and clean the vegetables, wrap the sardines in the grape leaves, skewer the lamb, etc. **Simplify:** Hummus is available ready-made in most major supermarkets these days. Wrap the sardines in aluminium foil instead of grape leaves. Use lamb chops instead; these don't need to go onto skewers (up the weight by about half, to compensate for the bones). **Leave out:** Leave out one of the salads.

Sauces, salsas and dressings

A sumptuous, fresh sauce can turn the most ordinary meal into something truly special. If nothing else says it, the sauce will a lot of thought and care has gone into your food. Which, of course is true... but does not mean that you have to spend hours in the kitchen. These clever little sauces and dressings are ready in no time and amazingly versatile. Success is guaranteed!

Making a sauce is to orchestrate flavours; you are the conductor. A good dressing can make or break a dish. A rich, velvety garlic wine sauce lends a feeling of unaccustomed luxury, and an artful drizzle of fresh strawberry dressing will turn a few slices of smoked chicken into an elegant starter. It's not for nought that the position of saucier or sauce maker is one of the most respected in the classic hierarchy of French restaurant kitchens. And, contrary to popular belief, you don't need to make it too complicated. Modern sauces are really not heavy and involved but rather very light and simple, while still being extremely flavourful. You don't have to worry about standing over the stove for hours watching some thick sauce bubble away. Sauces these days are centred round fresh, pure flavours which complement a dish without overwhelming it. (And though some sauces do indeed take a couple hours to cook, such as red wine sauces, there's nothing wrong with cheating a bit and sneaking in some bouillon concentrate from the jar.)

Exciting combinations

Here you can find recipes for sauces with a white or red wine base, as well as a vinaigrette, a dressing and a salsa. The greatest thing about these sauces is that, once you get the hang of them there is no limit to the flavour variations you can create with these simple bases. We have provided you with some of our own ideas, but the main thing is to be inspired by the ingredients themselves, or the season, or whoever is coming to dinner. It's also nice to create surprising combinations between the dish and the sauce that goes with it. A simple vinaigrette is very diverse and it's really a shame that most people reserve it for their salad only. Try a nice vinaigrette drizzled with pieces of olive and capers over a piece of grilled white fish, like seawolf. Or try an ostrich steak, grilled rare, topped with an out-of-this-world mushroom and pomegranate salsa. With a little practice, you can think up the perfect finishing touch for any dish!

Red wine garlic sauce

1 jar beef stock concentrate – 100 ml red wine –
16 cloves garlic – olive oil

1   Boil the beef stock concentrate and red wine down
    to one-third the original amount.
2   Place the cloves of garlic in a baking dish and pour
    in olive oil until they are completely covered.
3   Cook in a pre-heated oven at 200° C (400° F or gas
    mark 6) for fifteen minutes or until cooked through
    (the cloves will float to the top when done).
4   Add 6 cloves of the roasted garlic to the wine and
    beef stock mixture and puree with a hand-held
    blender. Save the remaining cloves for garnish. (Set
    the oil aside for dressings.)

Variation tips: instead of garlic, you can also add sautéed
mushrooms or a roasted sweet pepper (pureed), or a spoonful of honey and a bunch of thyme. For a creamier sauce,
simply whisk in some cold butter at the last minute.

Green vinaigrette

1 tbsp black olive – 1 tbsp capers – 1 tbsp parsley –
1 shallot – 1 tbsp white wine vinegar – 2 tbsp maize-
germ oil – 2 tbsp olive oil – 1 tsp sugar

Dissolve the sugar well in the vinegar, whisk in the oil
and stir in the other, finely chopped ingredients.

Variation tips: There's really no limit to the combinations to
be made between different oils and vinegars. Just remember
the proper proportions: three to four parts oil to one part
vinegar. You can add all imaginable herbs and seasonings to
these mixtures, such as parsley and garlic, rocket, dill or basil,
or one spoonful of honey to 2 spoonfuls of mustard, pureed
raspberries, sun-dried tomatoes...

Strawberry dressing

100 g (7 oz) strawberries – 1 egg yolk (pasteurised if desired) – 1 tbsp strawberry vinegar – 1 tsp mustard – 1 soup spoon bouillon – 1 tbsp honey – 1 dl (3.5 oz) maize-germ oil

With a hand-held blender, blend all the ingredients except the oil. Add this last, pouring in a slow, steady stream to help emulsify.

Variation tips: instead of strawberries, you can season the basic dressing with: 1 tbsp sherry (in this case you need herry vinegar instead of strawberry vinegar); pieces of walnut and chopped basil (use ½ dl (1.75 oz) olive oil and ½ dl (1.75 oz) nut oil); 1 roasted sweet pepper (use red wine vinegar); 3 or 4 sun-dried tomatoes (with olive oil and balsamic vinegar); or 100 g (3.5 oz) grated Parmesan cheese.

White wine and mustard sauce

1 jar fish stock concentrate – 100 ml (3.5 oz) white wine – 100 ml (3.5 oz) Noilly Prat vermouth – 2 tsp mustard – 2 anchovies

Put the stock concentrate, wine, Noilly Prat, cream and anchovies in a saucepan and boil down to half. Stir in the mustard, cook a minute or two longer, then strain through a fine sieve.

Variation tips: use this mixture, without the mustard and anchovies, as a base, then add chopped herbs (dill or coriander are delicious with fish). During the boil, you can infuse the sauce with all sorts of other ingredients, such as lemongrass – which will lend it a wonderfully fragrant, exotic aroma. If you have leftover scampi peels, you can fry them with a tbsp of tomato puree and to infuse the sauce (discard them afterwards). In this case, substitute cognac for the Noilly Prat.

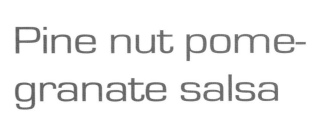

Pine nut pome-granate salsa

10 sautéed mushrooms – seeds of 1 pomegranate – 2 tbsp toasted pine nuts – 20 raisins – 1 lemon, peeled and diced – olive oil

Carefully mix all the ingredients, adding the diced lemon last. Very tasty with a 'carpaccio' of thinly sliced smoked chicken or other poultry, or with red meat or game.

Variation tips: Salsa is actually a chunky sauce made from (usually raw) ingredients such as tomato, red chili peppers, onion and garlic. Throw in some diced avocado for a twist, or a little lemon juice and fresh coriander leaves. Also very tasty: a coarsely chopped mango and half a coconut with a tablespoon of freshly grated ginger, a green chili pepper, fresh coriander leaves and mint.

party

Any excuse for a (cocktail) party!

Stylish, trendy, smart and sometimes a wee bit decadent: put a good cocktail in your friends' hands and suddenly it's a party! From the refreshing tang of the Mojito with its lime juice, mint leaves, rum and soda to the smooth dry kick of the Manhattan with its mix of whisky, vermouth and Angostura bitters. String up some colourful Chinese lanterns in your garden and scatter some tiki torches and hurricane lamps here and there. Just add some swinging music, a variety of easy-to-prepare yet exquisite snacks... and you have yourself a party you won't forget!

Cocktails are so undeniably tasty and festive that they are at once timeless and trendy. When done right, they can be a pleasure to the eye and a caress to the tongue (or vice-versa), can light up a room, and have intriguing and often racy names like 'Sex on the Beach', 'Barfly's Dream', 'Yellow Dragon', 'Between the Sheets' and 'Bloody Mary'. There is a healthy debate about the origins of the word 'cocktail'. Some tell a story about rooster feathers, literally 'cock tails', and pretty women named Coctel or Xochitl. Nobody really knows which story is the right one. In any case, it first appeared as a term for an alcoholic mixed drink in 1806, in the American newspaper "The Balance", meaning that cocktails have been around for at least two-hundred years... and are most definitely here to stay!

Simple luxury

Of course, there are trends. It was the disco age of the 1970s that brought us such inventive creations as the 'Tequila Sunrise' and 'Piña Colada'. Shooters had their heyday in the 1980s, and since the advent of the '90s to the present day, classic cocktails like the Martini and Cosmopolitan ('Cosmo' to the initiated) are experiencing a renaissance. These days old standbys like these have their place next to the new wave of drinks which are continually popping up in the world's hipper watering holes, many of them outlandish twists on the originals. Modern cocktails are luxurious, fruity yet savoury, not too heavy and not overly sweet. And, above all, refreshingly uncomplicated. You need flavourful fresh ingredients and good-quality spirits, meaning the various flavours should be recognisable. All the ingredients should complement each other without one becoming muddled by the other. If you aim to invent your own cocktail, the byword here is simplicity. Get inspiration from tried and true classics that you and your friends all enjoy drinking. It might just happen that by the end of the evening you'll have discovered your ideal mix, including a stylish garnish and a suitably evocative name!

Tip: Aubergines should be firm to the touch and have a shiny, unblemished peel. Do not use too much oil, as the aubergines will absorb most of this.

Aubergine rollatini

1 aubergine, sliced into thin strips
2 tbsp green olives, pitted and finely chopped
1/2 tbsp pine nuts, finely chopped
2 anchovies, finely chopped
1/2 tbsp capers, finely chopped
2 tbsp Parmesan cheese, grated

1 Salt the aubergine and set it aside to infuse for 30 minutes.
2 Rinse well and pat dry. Cook the strips in a grill pan for approx. 2 minutes or until brown grill marks appear.
3 Combine the remaining ingredients.
4 Spread this mixture over the aubergine slices and roll them up. Stick a toothpick through each one to hold it closed.

Sharp cheese and tomato on toast

4 thick slices whole-grain bread
5 vine tomatoes
60 g (2 oz) Roquefort
40 g (1.4 oz) fresh goat's cheese
1 beefsteak or other stewing tomato, peeled, seeded and diced
1 tsp red wine vinegar
4 tbsp (Greek) olive oil
sea salt and freshly grated pepper
1 spring onion, very finely chopped
2 tbsp parsley, finely chopped
2 tbsp basil, finely chopped
12 black olives

1 Toast the bread in an oven at 150° C (300° F or gas mark 2) for 30 minutes or until dry and crisp.

2 Grate the vine tomatoes on a vegetable grater as far as the skin, straining the resulting pulp through a sieve.

3 Combine the Roquefort and goat's cheese and mix to a smooth consistency.

4 Stir the diced beefsteak tomatoes and wine vinegar into the tomato pulp.

5 Place the toast on four small plates and drizzle with 2 tbsp oil. Generously spread with the tomato blend. Sprinkle with salt and pepper.

6 Top with minced onion, parsley, basil, cheese and olives. Drizzle with the remaining oil.

for approx. 15 pieces
350 g (12 oz) tinned crab
meat, drained
2 eggs
2 spring onions,
finely chopped
1 tbsp crème fraîche
2 tsp sweet chili sauce
100 g (3.5 oz) floury (mealy)
cooking potatoes, boiled
1 tbsp coriander (cilantro),
chopped

For the avocado salsa:
2 vine tomatoes, cored,
seeded and diced
½ red onion,
very finely very chopped
1 avocado, diced
½ red chili pepper,
very finely chopped
1 clove of garlic,
very finely chopped
juice of ½ lime
2 tbsp coriander (cilantro),
chopped
oil for frying
salt and pepper

Crab cakes with avocado salsa

1 Combine all the ingredients for the crab cakes and mix to a stiff and even consistency. Season with salt and pepper to taste. Using your hands, shape the mix into balls the size of a golf ball. Flatten these to a thickness of about ½ cm (0.2").
2 For the salsa, combine the diced tomato, red onion, avocado, chili, garlic, lime juice and coriander. Salt lightly.
3 Fry the crab cakes in a generous amount of oil until brown on each side, approx. 3 minutes per side. Place on paper towels to drain and serve with the avocado salsa.

Port-infused figs with Stilton and chives

for 8 pieces

300 ml (10.5 oz) port

10 g (0.35 oz) sugar

4 fresh figs

200 g (7 oz) Stilton, crumbled

1 tbsp fresh chives, chopped

1 Heat the sugar with the port until totally dissolved.

2 Pour over the figs and set aside to marinate for 8 hours.

3 Remove the figs from the port, pat them dry and halve them. Cover each half with the Stilton and sprinkle with chives.

Party food

Whether you have plenty of time for putting together snacks, or hardly any at all, try to avoid those boring bowls of crisps and salted nuts. Replace these time-worn clichés with a few stylish and simple cocktail snacks, making sure you have plenty to go round. Better to have a whole heap of two or three types of food then ten different things for each person. Three is, after all, the magic number here: one snack with meat, one with fish and one vegetarian option. Set out small dishes of marinated olives and savoury nuts for the side (see p.142). Meatballs, crab cakes and the like often disappear with astonishing speed, so aim for about five per person.

Party time!

Spicy prawn skewers with coriander mayonnaise

for 8 people

24 small prawns, unpeeled
juice of ½ grapefruit
2 cloves of garlic, pressed
1 red chili pepper, seeded and very finely chopped
3 tbsp olive oil
1.5 dl (5.25 oz) water
100 g (3.5 oz) snow peas
2 grapefruits, cut into segments

for the coriander mayonnaise:

4 tbsp mayonnaise
4 tbsp crème fraîche
15 coriander (cilantro) leaves, finely chopped
sprinkle of lemon juice

1 Peel the prawns (save the peels) and de-vein them with a paring knife.
2 Combine the grapefruit juice, garlic, red chili pepper and 2 tbsp olive oil and place the prawns in this mixture to marinate for at least 1 hour. Simmer the prawns in the marinade for 5 minutes on medium heat.
3 Meanwhile, fry the prawn peels in 1 tablespoon oil on high heat until they colour. Add the water.
4 Boil the liquid down until it has almost all evaporated, then drain the peels in a sieve, pressing the juice out with a spoon. Discard the peels and combine the juice with the mayonnaise, crème fraîche, coriander and the lemon juice, stirring to a smooth sauce. Set aside to chill.
5 Blanch the snow peas in plenty of boiling salted water (they should be just tender). Carefully split the pods in half lengthwise.
6 Fold each half around a prawn or grapefruit segment, then slide these onto skewers. Serve with the coriander mayonnaise.

Danish meatballs

1 shallot, very finely chopped
2 tbsp butter or oil
500 g (17.5 oz) minced (ground) beef
1 egg
3 tbsp pastry flour
salt and freshly grated pepper
pinch of nutmeg
200 ml (7 oz) beef jus
1-2 tbsp corn starch
250 ml (1 cup) yoghurt, room temperature
1 tbsp mustard
2 tbsp dill, chopped
1 tbsp tarragon

1 Sauté the shallot in 1 tbsp butter until translucent, removing from the heat when done.
2 Combine the mincemeat, shallot, egg, pastry flour, salt, pepper and nutmeg in a mixing bowl.
3 Mix and knead well, then shape the mixture into meatballs and fry in the remaining butter until brown.
4 Pour in the jus and cook another 10 minutes or until done throughout.
5 Combine the yoghurt and corn starch and add this to the meatballs.
6 Combine with the mustard and stir to a smooth sauce, sprinkling with the dill and tarragon to finish.

Indian sandwich

4 pieces of naan bread (or 4 slices of white sandwich bread)
200 g (8.75 oz) grated cheese
100 g (3.5 oz) soft goat's cheese
12 slices of bacon
6 tbsp diced tomatoes
2 tbsp olive oil
1 red chili pepper, seeded and sliced
1 green chili pepper, seeded and sliced
1 shallot, very finely chopped
2 tbsp coriander (cilantro)

1 Make a sandwich out of two pieces of naan (or two slices of sandwich bread), the cheese, goat's cheese and bacon.
2 Toast for about 4 minutes in a pre-heated oven at 220° C (425° F or gas mark 7).
3 Combine the remaining ingredients and use this mixture to top the naan with the cheese.
4 Cover the naan sandwich with the two other pieces of naan and briefly toast once more.
5 Cut the sandwich into triangles.

Tip: For spicy food lovers, serve this with a bit of chili paste, such as Indonesian sambal badjak. This type of sambal is made with more onion than some varieties, giving it a sweeter and milder flavour.

Javanese meatballs

For approx. 32 pieces
750 g (1.66 lbs) sweet potatoes, diced
750 g (1.66 lbs) minced (ground) beef
3 eggs
6 shallots, very finely chopped
6 cloves of garlic, very finely chopped
6 cm (2.4 ") fresh ginger root, grated
1 tsp trasi (prawn paste), crushed smooth
3 tsp palm sugar
6 tbsp Indonesian ketjap manis
1 red chili pepper, very finely chopped
3 tbsp ground coriander
4 tsp ground cumin
1 tsp ground cinnamon
6 dl (2 oz) peanut oil for frying

1 Boil the diced sweet potato in lightly salted water (15-20 minutes). Strain and mash until smooth. Allow to cool slightly.

2 Mix with the minced meat (ground beef), eggs, shallots, garlic, ginger, trasi, palm sugar, ketjap manis, red chili pepper, spices and a little salt. The mixture should be firm enough not to stick to your fingers.

3 Shape the mixture into approx. 32 balls, each the size of a walnut.

4 Heat the oil in a frying pan. Fry the balls in the oil for approx. 5 minutes or until crispy. Remove from the pan with a spatula or slotted spoon and place on paper towels to drain. Serve hot or cold.

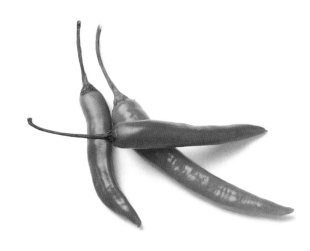

Savoury nuts

Toss 500 grams (17.5 oz) mixed, shelled nuts and seeds (try cashews, pistachios, pecans, walnuts, peanuts, sunflower and pumpkin seeds) with a generous dash of olive oil, two teaspoons of salt, freshly grated black pepper, two tablespoons brown sugar and one tablespoon curry powder or mixed spices (mustard, ground cumin, coriander and paprika, for example). Spread the nuts out on a baking sheet and roast in a preheated oven on low to medium heat, approx. 150° C (300° F or gas mark 2), until they turn a light golden brown (keep an eye on them – they burn easily!).

Thai crab salad

Thai crab salad

For 8 pieces

1 red chili pepper,
seeded and very finely chopped
1 clove of garlic, pressed
2 cm (0.8") lemongrass,
finely chopped
juice and zest (grated rind)
of ½ lime
1 tbsp fish sauce
100 ml (3.5 oz) coconut milk
(tinned)
1 heaped tsp sugar
1 shallot or spring onion,
finely chopped
250 g (8.75 oz) crab meat,
fresh or tinned
½ bunch basil, torn into strips
½ bunch fresh coriander (cilantro),
finely chopped,
plus extra for garnishing
8 slices of toast

1 Combine the chili pepper, garlic, lemongrass, lime juice and lime zest, fish sauce, coconut milk and sugar, mixing well. The sugar should completely dissolve.

2 Add the shallot. Salt to taste.

3 Add the crab meat, basil and coriander. Mix well.

4 Top the pieces of toast with the salad. Sprinkle with a little fresh coriander and more chili pepper if necessary.

Tip: Only use the tender centre of the lemongrass, discarding the rough outer stalk (or save this to infuse Thai curry sauces). Make sure there are no pieces of shell in the crab meat, especially in the case of fresh crab, by feeling with your fingers.

Tip 2: A very attractive presentation for this dish is to serve it in crisp lettuce leaves; 'Little Gem' is a good variety for this.

Chicken tikka

For 8 people

750 g (1.66 lbs) chicken fillet, in strips

for the marinade:

5 tbsp peanut oil

3½ tbsp red wine vinegar

1 onion, very finely chopped

5 cloves of garlic, very finely chopped

3 cm (1.2 ") ginger root, finely chopped

2 tbsp ground cumin

2 tsp ground coriander

1 tbsp ground cardamom

1 tsp ground cinnamon

1 tsp ground cloves

20 black peppercorns, crushed

3 tsp salt

1 tbsp tomato puree

Tip: If you're running short on time, simply combine two table-spoons of curry paste from the jar with the oil and vinegar.

1 Puree all the ingredients for the marinade to a smooth paste in a food processor.
2 Pour the marinade over the chicken and mix well. Chill for 4-5 hours in the refrigerator, covered.
3 Heat a grill pan and cover with aluminium foil. Place about half the chicken strips in a single layer on top of the foil (you do not need to pat them dry first).
4 Grill for approx. 10 minutes on each side.
5 Keep the cooked chicken warm while you grill the second batch in the same manner. Serve immediately.

Stuffed papaya

for 8 people
4 small papayas
250 g (8.75 oz) hearts of palm, sliced
2 mangos, diced
½ melon, diced
½ pineapple, diced
2 passion fruits

for the dressing:
juice of 1 lime
2 tsp honey
1 tsp mustard
2 tbsp mango chutney
50 ml (1.75 oz) olive oil

1 Halve the papayas lengthwise. Scoop out the pits
   and carefully cut away the peel. Keep the peel in
   one piece for filling.
2 Dice the papaya and combine with the hearts of
   palm, mango, melon and pineapple. Halve the
   passion fruits and stir the pulp into the fruit salad.
3 Make the dressing: combine all the ingredients and
   mix well. Toss the salad with the dressing. Chill for
   1 hour, stir, then fill the papaya halves with the fruit.

The foundation

You can always stick to cocktails which are stirred (not shaken) but a true authentic cocktail party really must have a classic metal shaker with a built-in strainer. The ingredients go into the shaker together with some ice cubes. Shaking both mixes the drink and chills it at the same time. When sufficiently shaken, pour it through the strainer and into a glass, keeping the ice behind. Mojitos and the like require a muddler for the limes. You can create some deliciously frothy cocktails with a countertop or handheld blender. An extra-long bar spoon comes in handy for stirring tall drinks and a small measuring cup is indispensable for precise measuring of ingredients.

The most popular spirits are whisky, rum, tequila, vodka, gin, cognac (or brandy) and various liqueurs. Just three or four bottles from this list already make a pretty good drinks (liquor) cabinet. For the best cocktails, of course, you will need the best spirits, but this does not mean you always have to go for the most expensive either. Ask at your local off-license (or liquor store) for advice. Off-brand bottles can be just great, though they are sometimes more watered down than the well-known brands, which makes them less flavourful. You can tell by what proof they are. A little comparison is always a good idea. Don't forget that you might have guests who have to drive or simply don't want to drink: choose one or more non-alcoholic drinks for them. Have a look at p. 50. Get everything ready in advance which you will need: squeeze plenty of citrus juice, make the simple syrup, freeze some ice cubes, get plenty of garnish ready and stick all the bottles in the refrigerator to chill. Now just throw together a few tasty snacks and you're ready to go!

Fruity rum punch

40 ml (1.4 oz) rum – 50 ml (1.75 oz) pineapple juice – 5 dl (1 pint) guava juice – 50 ml (1.75 oz) mango juice – finely grated rind (zest) of 1 lime – 75 g (2.5 oz) cane sugar – 1 papaya, diced – ½ pineapple, diced small – ½ melon, diced – 1 mango, diced

1 Mix the rum with the fruit juice and lime zest. Set 1 dl (3.5 oz) juice aside.
2 Heat this with the cane sugar until the sugar has completely dissolved. Add this mixture to the remaining juices; chill for several hours.
3 Mix the fruit and place in a punch bowl or portion into glasses. Pour in the rum mix and serve with a straw and spoon.

Grappasorbet spoom

50 ml (1.75 oz) water – 150 g (5.25 oz) white castor sugar – 2 tbsp ginger syrup – 4 tbsp grappa – champagne or sparkling white wine

1. Bring the water and sugar to a boil and cook until the sugar is totally dissolved.
2. Remove from the heat and let the mixture cool, then add the ginger syrup and grappa. Pour into a plastic container.
3. Keep the mixture in the coldest part of the freezer for about 5 hours. Stir once every hour with a fork as it freezes.
4. Chill 4 glasses. Place a scoop of sorbet into each glass and top off with champagne.

Campari Orange

25 ml (0.9 oz) vodka
10 ml (0.35 oz) Grand Marnier
10 ml (0.35 oz) Campari
90 ml (3 oz) fresh-squeezed orange juice
dash of iced tea
orange slice
ice cubes

1 Stir all the ingredients together and pour into
   a tumbler.
2 Add ice and garnish with a slice of orange.

Glasswork

A beautiful glass needs but little extra garnish. The glass you need of course depends on the cocktail. The classic cocktail glass, used for Martinis and Manhattans among other drinks, contains roughly 80 ml (2.8 oz) and is wide-brimmed. Other cocktails look quite attractive in a small tumbler or whisky glass, or a nice tulip-shaped wine glass. Cocktails containing fruit juice are often served in a tall Collins glass.

Candied citrus peel

It does take some time but the result is wonderful: candied citrus peel. Place thin strips of lemon, lime or orange peel in cold water and bring to a boil. Strain, add more cold water and return to a boil. In another saucepan dissolve 250 g (8.8 oz) (1 cup) sugar in 2.5 dl (1 cup) water. Place the peels in this mixture for 5 minutes (keeping it at a gentle simmer). Sprinkle the peels with coarse-grain sugar and place them aside to dry. If you wrap the strips of peel around chopsticks to dry, you will end up with attractive curlicues. A festive garnish for any cocktail.

Sugar rims

It's easy to rim a cocktail glass in sugar: first dip the rim in lemon or lime juice, then press it into the sugar (or salt, for dry cocktails and margaritas). Shake off the excess sugar and let it dry briefly. If you want to get funky, add a drop of food colouring to the sugar to get a wacky green, blue or red rim. (Over the top, but pretty impressive all the same...)

Mojito

60 ml (2 oz) white rum
fresh mint leaves
1 tsp simple syrup
½ lime
ice cubes
soda water
mint sprig for garnishing

1 Muddle the mint leaves and simple syrup in a Collins glass. Squeeze the lime over this mixture.
2 Add rum and ice and stir well.
3 Top off with soda water, stir gently and garnish with a mint sprig.

Tip 1: Serve the cocktail in a tumbler with plenty of crushed ice and a short straw if desired. It looks so nice with the lime and mint leaves that any more garnish would really be too much.

Tip 2: Instead of rum use cachaça, the national drink of Brazil – now you have a Caipirinha. Cachaça (pronounced "ka'shassa"), like rum, is derived from sugarcane. The difference is that it comes from the whole, green stalk, while the scraps left after sugar production are often what goes into rum. This spirit tastes somewhat cleaner and fruitier than normal rum.

Strawberry Dream

50 ml (1.75 oz) cachaça – 3 strawberries – 2 tbsp sugar – 2 lime wedges – crushed ice – strawberry for garnishing

1 Muddle the strawberries in a glass, add the sugar and lime and muddle once again.
2 Add ice and cachaça. Stir well.
3 Serve on the rocks in a tumbler. Garnish with a strawberry and stick a short straw in the glass.

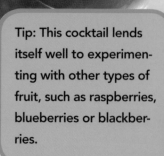

Tip: This cocktail lends itself well to experimenting with other types of fruit, such as raspberries, blueberries or blackberries.

Gold leaf

Edible gold leaf is a glamorous garnish for a truly deluxe cocktail. A few shreds on top of a drink gives the cocktail an irresistible glow. You can find gold leaf in specialty chocolate shops, where they use it to decorate their finest confections. Don't handle it too much – the stuff melts fast!

Nice 'n' ice cold

Ice is an indispensable part of any cocktail evening: a whole lot of it. You almost always need more than you think, so buy a couple of bags, or freeze plenty of trays beforehand. Some cocktails require cracked ice. If your freezer doesn't automatically dispense this, as some do, there's always the old-fashioned way: put ice cubes in a tea towel and hit it with a hammer until the ice cubes fracture. If you keep hitting, you'll end up with crushed ice. You can also buy special ice-crushers which do this for you; keep your eyes open the next time you go to the junk shop and you might just find an antique crank-handled version – these work too! You can create unique decorative ice cubes by freezing a piece of fruit or flower petal in each cube. You can also fill the ice tray with fruit juice for a sweet and refreshing twist. It goes without saying that these only belong in certain drinks!

Garnishes: subtle chic – or retro kitsch?

The days when you ordered a cocktail and it came with half a fruit stuck on the rim are over. Modern garnishes are subtle and stylish: a twist of citrus peel, an olive or one nice piece of fruit. The flavour, of course, must suit the cocktail: for a cocktail made with raspberry liqueur, stick two fresh raspberries on a cocktail pick for an easy and attractive garnish which also serves as an immediate indicator of the drink's ingredients. Slide some fruit onto a cocktail pick and place this in the drink or balance it on the rim. It's easy to garnish with a thicker slice of fruit by making an incision halfway through (not far enough to actually cut it in two). It's better to use fresh fruit if you have the chance; this tastes and looks better than anything from a tin. Two coloured straws which go with the colour of the drink are also a nice addition, or a single edible flower floated on top of the drink. If you're in a retro mood, don't go halfway – go all out! Collect as many crazy cocktail umbrellas, swizzle sticks, brightly coloured straws and ice moulds as you can, assemble the most extravagant fruit decorations and let yourself go crazy!

Manhattan

Tip: Pour the drink into stylish cocktail glasses and garnish with one or two maraschino cherries and a nice cocktail pick, or simply a twist of lemon peel.

60 ml (2 oz) rye whisky – 30 ml (1 oz) sweet vermouth – 3 dashes angostura bitters – drops of maraschino juice – one maraschino cherry

1 Stir all the ingredients together in a mixing glass.
2 Pour through a strainer into a cocktail glass. Put a cherry into each glass.

Pesto & tapenade

The ideal welcome snack, appetiser, pacifier and mood-setter. Home-made tapenades and pestos are at the top of the list of those clever little details which really round off a meal or party.

It's always the little things that make a difference. It's nice to offer your guests a tasty snack as soon as they arrive. It comes across as very hospitable and has the added bonus of creating a relaxed atmosphere, with all the nibbling helping to break the ice. Some good home-made tapenade or pesto is ideal for this purpose. Who isn't crazy about those appetising little spreads, so surprisingly full of flavour? Just set a basket of crispy bread out with one or two kinds of tapenade or pesto, maybe some marinated olives, and let the guests help themselves. This will also keep people happy if you end up in the kitchen longer than planned. You can make everything a day in advance – it only takes a second. And because most people only know pesto from the jars in the supermarket, they will be quite impressed that you've made your own from scratch!

Classic or contemporary?

Officially, there is only one pesto (it comes from Genoa and is made with basil, olive oil, pecorino cheese, garlic and pine nuts), just like there's only one tapenade (from Provence, ingredients: black olives, capers, anchovies and olive oil). Nobody these days is going to reprimand you for breaking with tradition, not even if they happen to be from Genoa or Provence. All sorts of herbs and other ingredients can be ground into a delicious spread. Decide for yourself whether to go the old-fashioned route or to try something new.

Anybody not too pressed for time can pay homage to a time-honoured tradition and put the old mortar and pestle to work. Though it's often claimed that crushing the ingredients relea-

ses more flavour than grinding them, you will probably want to just throw everything in a food processor, where a simple press of a button will create a nice smooth puree – but not too smooth (try for a handcrafted consistency). Pour the olive oil in last, adding just enough to give the mixture a spreadable texture. Presentation is everything: use attractive little dishes and garnish the pestos and tapenades with nuts, olives or a sprig of herbs.

Spicy coriander pesto

1 red chili pepper – 4 cloves of garlic – 1 bunch coriander (cilantro) – 50 g (1.75 oz) pumpkin seeds – 1 tbsp lemon juice – 100 g (3.5 oz) manchego (or any other mild sheep's cheese), grated – olive oil

Remove the seeds and core from the chili (unless your guests can handle some heat, then leave it in). Blend the chili in the food processor, add garlic, coriander and pumpkin seeds and puree. Mix in the grated cheese and enough olive oil to make the mixture spreadable. Add salt, pepper and lemon juice to taste.

Tuna tapenade

100 g (3.5 oz) black olives – 100 g (3.5 oz) oil-cured tuna (tinned) – 4 anchovies – 1 tsp mustard – 1 tbsp capers – basil, parsley, rocket or any other green herbs you have on hand.

Place all the ingredients in a food processor and puree until semi-smooth, adding salt, pepper or olive oil to taste.

153

Sun-dried tomato pesto

8 pieces oil-cured sun-dried tomatoes – 50 g (1.75 oz)
Parmesan cheese, grated – 3 tbsp pine nuts, briefly
toasted in a dry pan – 1 bunch of basil – 3 tbsp olive oil

1   Blend the tomato, pine nuts and basil in the
food processor.
2   Stir in the cheese.
3   Add enough oil to make the mixture spreadable.
4   Taste and add salt and pepper if needed.

Fresh artichoke tapenade

2 large fresh artichokes – 100 g (3.5 oz) green olives –
1 bunch basil – 100 g (3.5 oz) Mahon (or any semi-hard
cheese of your choice), grated – 1 tbsp capers – 1 tsp
lemon juice – 2 tbsp olive oil

1 Boil the artichokes for approx. 20 minutes or until
tender (they are done when a leaf comes off easily
in your hand). Remove the leaves and inner hairs,
setting the nice leaves aside for later.
2 Coarsely puree the artichoke bottoms with the
remaining ingredients. Season with lemon juice, salt
and pepper.
3 Serve the leaves with the tapenade as dip (the soft
bottom part of the leave is also edible).

Wild mushroom tapenade

250 g (8.75 oz) wild mushrooms, sautéed and cooled
-100 g (3.5 oz) green olives – 1 bunch of parsley –
2 tbsp olive oil

1 Coarsely blend the sautéed mushrooms, olives and
  parsley in the food processor.
2 Add 2 tbsp olive oil, or enough oil to make the
  mixture nice and spreadable.
3 Add salt and pepper to taste.

Pestos and tapenades have many more uses than just as a spread for baguettes or crostini. Try them as an original side dish, sauce or seasoning. Serve as pasta sauce or with risotto, meat or fish, or put a scoop into soup right before serving.

banquet

Sultry summers, big banquets

You want to serve up a really festive meal this time round? If you're catering to your best friends, it doesn't have to be very formal, but by making the meal extra chic and luxurious, you will be presenting them with something truly special. You've thought about every detail: the table is brilliantly set with your nicest dishes, fresh tapers and glittering crystal. And the tongue-teasing banquet you're about to dish up is already done for the most part. A little 'finishing touch' and you can take a load off and eat as one of the guests!

A nice moment to toss all culinary inhibitions to the wind, whatever the occasion – a silver anniversary, an important jubilee or special birthday, or perhaps a long-awaited graduation? If you have friends who think they know everything about cooking and haute cuisine, this is your chance to pull out all the stops and really impress them: from caviar to sweetbread, from duck confit to dried fruit slices! Of course, you don't really have to go over the top, especially if some of the guests might be scared off by too much finery, or you have a, shall we say, less than infinite budget to work with. You will be surprised at the luxurious and refined four-course meal you can put together with the simplest ingredients and a little wine. It will be an occasion to remember.

The never-ending meal

Are you and your friends looking forward to a long, balmy summer evening of wining and dining on delicious canapés? Why not make an eight-course meal of it? Of course, each course will consist of only a small amuse-bouche, but presented in the most exquisite fashion. This will turn the meal into a series of flavour experiences, a little something for the senses – not enough to make you feel like you overdid it by the end of the evening. Serve suitable wines, also in the appropriate quantities. And make sure you have plenty of plates!

Tip: The trout will taste best if you cure it yourself in a smoker or with a disposable smoking bag you simply place in the oven (available at most major kitchen stores). Take 100 grams of coarse sea salt and 2 tablespoons hickory dust (you should be able to find this wherever grilling accessories are sold). Pat 400 g (14 oz) of trout dry, rub with the salt and place in a cool spot, covered, for 2 hours. Rinse and smoke the trout for 10 minutes.

Smoked trout with ginger dressing

400 g (14 oz) good-quality smoked trout (not too salty)

For the dressing:

12 tbsp olive oil

1 tsp curry

2 tsp lime zest (finely grated rind)

5 tbsp lime juice

1 tsp fresh ginger, finely grated

1 tsp sesame oil

sea salt

1 Heat the olive oil on a low heat and add the curry, stirring until dissolved. Add the remaining ingredients for the dressing. Heat the mixture on a low heat.

2 Divide the fish into four portions and give each one a generous drizzle of the warm dressing.

3 Serve on a salad of frisée, grated carrot and chopped macadamia nuts with a neutral vinaigrette, or with boiled asparagus.

Spring salad with polenta croutons

100 g (3.5 oz) haricots verts,
blanched until tender
1 green onion, sliced
½ bunch parsley, finely chopped
½ bunch basil, in strips
2 tomatoes, sliced
100 g (3.5 oz) Parmesan cheese,
shaved (use a cheese slicer)
1 tbsp olive oil
½ tbsp balsamic vinegar

For the croutons:
100 g (3.5 oz) vegetable stock
100 g (3.5 oz) tomato juice
100 g (3.5 oz) polenta (corn meal)

1 For the croutons, heat the bouillon and the juice, then stir in the polenta.
2 Boil this for 15 minutes, stirring often, or according to the directions on the package.
3 On a large cutting board or other surface spread the polenta out to a layer approx. 1 cm (0.4 ") thick.
4 Allow to cool. When stiff, cut the sheet into nice even cubes. Preheat the oven to 180° C (350° F or gas mark 4).
5 Bake the croutons for 30 minutes or until crispy. Turn regularly.
6 Combine all the ingredients for the salad and garnish with the croutons.
7 Drizzle with the oil and balsamic vinegar.

30 cloves of garlic
50 g (1.75 oz) butter
1.5 l (3 pints) chicken stock
salt and freshly ground pepper
pinch of freshly grated nutmeg
5 egg yolks
1 dl (3.5 oz) cream
3-4 tbsp olive oil
6 pieces of toast

Garlic soup

1 Sauté the whole garlic cloves in the butter, not long enough to actually brown them.
2 When the garlic cloves have softened add the bouillon and simmer the soup on a low heat for about 20 minutes.
3 Puree the soup with a handheld blender and season with salt, pepper and freshly grated nutmeg to taste.
4 Combine the egg yolks and cream and add a cup of soup, from the stove. Stir well and add the mixture to the soup. Return the soup to the heat and keep at a simmer. Do not boil.
5 Froth with a handheld blender and serve with toast.

Festive aperitif

Offer a refreshing cocktail about half an hour before the meal; this will whet your guests' appetite, especially if you serve a small canapé on the side. An aperitif or before-dinner drink is usually dry or semi-dry in flavour and not too complicated as far as the ingredients go. (Compared to an after-dinner drink, which is generally sweeter or creamier.) The Manhattan (see p. 149) and the Mojito (p. 147) are two examples of a tasty aperitif. Whatever the case, serve the cocktails ice-cold; you can even put the glasses in the freezer an hour beforehand to get them nice and frosty.

Cocktails with tonic water are also very well-suited to drinking before dinner. An ice-cold gin and tonic with a slice of lime is a true pleasure when taken on your garden terrace of a sunny afternoon, wonderfully refreshing and appetising. Or try your hand at the 'Portonic', a popular Portuguese aperitif. Simply mix equal parts dry white port and tonic (both ice-cold) in a Collins glass with a few ice cubes and lemon or lime wedges. This drink goes so well with fresh figs and Parma ham. Make two crosswise incisions into the fig from the stem to just above the bottom, then fold it open by pulling apart the resulting four segments. Drizzle with a little balsamic vinegar and top with a slice of Parma ham. Aperitifs made with sparkling wine can also be very festive. The famous Venetian 'Bellini' is one of these. To make a Bellini, briefly blanch a white peach in boiling water, so that the peel can be easily removed, then puree the pulp. Place two tablespoons of this puree into a champagne flute and fill with chilled Prosecco (a dry, frisante wine from the area around Venice). Another good idea we can thank the Italians for: 'Negroni Sbagliato' from Milan. Mix two parts Spumante (sparkling wine from northern Italy) with one part red vermouth and one part Campari and serve with an orange slice. A bittersweet salad makes a splendid accompaniment: cut an endive into strips and toss these with mandarin orange segments, chopped pistachios and a dressing made from one tablespoon orange juice, one tablespoon olive oil and one teaspoon white wine vinegar. Serve this in over-sized spoons or in an attractive endive leaf.

Tip: Blanch the vegetables in advance, then they will only need to cook a few minutes (you can do this while the sweetbreads cook).

Veal sweetbreads with Madeira sauce

1 For the sauce, gently sauté the onion, carrot and celery in the oil. Add the beef stock concentrate, Madeira and cream and simmer for 30 minutes.

2 Strain the sauce and season with salt and pepper to taste. Set aside or keep simmering if you desire a thicker sauce.

3 Sprinkle the sweetbread with salt, pepper and flour.

4 Fry in butter for 2 minutes or until brown.

5 Stir-fry the asparagus until they are hot and tender throughout.

6 Heat the sauce if necessary. Divide the asparagus over 4 plates, top with the sweetbread slices and pour on the sauce.

400 g (14 oz) veal sweetbreads, cleaned and cut into 1 cm (0.4") slices
500 g (17.5 oz) white asparagus, peeled and cut into 4 cm (1.5") strips
1 tbsp flour
salt and pepper
butter for frying

For the sauce:
½ onion, thinly sliced
½ carrot, thinly sliced
¼ celery stalk, thinly sliced
1 380 ml (~13 oz) jar of beef stock concentrate
2 dl (7 oz) madeira
2 dl (7 oz) cream
1 tbsp olive oil
salt and pepper

Chunky prawn mousse with yoghurt

100 g (3.5 oz) North Sea prawns, coarsely chopped
1 tbsp yoghurt
2 tbsp mayonnaise (see recipe)
juice of 1/2 lemon
1 tbsp basil, minced
1 tomato, cut into ½ cm (0.2") slices
salt and freshly ground pepper

For the mayonnaise:
1 egg yolk
1 tsp gherkin juice or white wine vinegar
1 tsp mustard
1 tsp lemon juice
1 cup maize-germ oil
salt and pepper

1 For the mayonnaise, mix the egg yolk, gherkin juice, mustard and lemon juice, either with a handheld blender or whisking continually by hand.

2 Add the oil a few drops at a time. Whisk, or blend vigorously until all of the oil has emulsified. Add salt and pepper to taste.

3 Mix 2 tablespoons of the mayonnaise with the yoghurt, lemon juice and basil. Stir in the prawns.

4 Fry the tomato slices on a hot grill pan until there are grill marks on both sides. Sprinkle with salt and freshly ground pepper.

5 Put a tomato slice and a spoonful of prawn mousse on each plate. Or serve on an oversized 'Amuse spoon'.

1 l (1 qt) vegetable stock
4 white asparagus stalks,
peeled (save the peels), cut
into small pieces
4 scallops, thinly sliced
1 tbsp garden cress

1 Place the scallop slices into
   4 shallow bowls.
2 Heat the vegetable stock
   and place the asparagus
   peels in this to infuse for
   ten minutes. Pour through
   a sieve and return to the
   stove, heating through well.
3 When the stock is quite hot,
   add the asparagus pieces
   and let them steep for
   4 minutes.
4 Ladle the hot stock over the
   scallops and garnish with
   garden cress.

Asparagus soup with scallops

4 x150 g (5.25 oz) hake fillets
4 tbsp flour
1 tsp curry powder
2 tbsp olive oil
salt and pepper

For the ratatouille:
8 tbsp olive oil
500 g (17.5 oz) aubergine,
cut into cubes
400 g (14 oz) courgette,
cut into cubes
2 sweet red peppers
400 g (14 oz) tomatoes,
seeded and chopped
2 red chili peppers
2 onions, chopped
4 anchovies, chopped
2 cloves of garlic, chopped
1 sprig of thyme
2 tbsp balsamic vinegar
100 g (3.5 oz) black olives
2 tbsp flat-leaf parsley, chopped
2 tbsp pine nuts

Fried hake fillets with ratatouille

1 Preheat the oven to 160 °C (325° F or gas mark 3). Fry the aubergine cubes in 2 tbsp of olive oil for approx. 3 minutes on high heat, or until they begin to brown. Place in a baking dish.

2 Repeat with the courgette, followed by the sweet pepper together with the tomatoes and chili. Place everything in the baking dish.

3 Put the same pan on low heat and sauté the onion with the anchovies and garlic until the onion has softened and the anchovies have totally disintegrated.

4 Add this to the vegetables in the baking dish. Stir well, then add the thyme and vinegar and season with salt and pepper to taste.

5 Bake for 20 minutes, covered.

6 Sprinkle the flour over a plate and season generously with salt, pepper and the curry powder. Heat the olive oil in a frying pan, coat the fillets in the flour mixture and fry on high heat until golden brown (about 2 minutes on each side).

7 Place the fillets on top of the ratatouille for the last 5 minutes of the cooking time, adding the olives at the same time.

8 Sprinkle with parsley and pine nuts. This is delicious with saffron rice.

Risotto with peas and rocket sauce

400 g (14 oz) risotto rice
25 g (0.7 oz) butter
1 small onion,
very finely chopped
1 l (1 qt) vegetable stock,
hot
200 g (7 oz) peas,
cooked until tender
100 g (3.5 oz) Parmesan
cheese, grated

For the cucumber cakes:
1 small cucumber,
finely grated
approx. 80 g (2.8 oz) flour
juice of ½ lemon
1 egg
clump of butter

For the rocket sauce:
2 tbsp white wine
2 dl (7 oz) vegetable
stock
2 dl (7 oz) cream
50 g (1.75 oz) pine nuts,
toasted
1 bunch of rocket,
finely chopped

1 For the risotto, heat the butter and sauté the onion until translucent. Add the rice and continue stirring until the grains of rice also turn translucent.

2 Add a dash of hot bouillon to the rice and continue cooking. Add another dash of bouillon once this has been completely absorbed by the rice.

3 Repeat until the rice is done, but not dry (risotto must be sticky and slightly fluid).

4 Meanwhile, prepare the sauce: boil the wine, bouillon and cream down to half. Add the rocket and pine nuts and heat briefly. Do not boil past this point. Taste and add salt and pepper if needed.

5 Stir the cheese and the peas into the risotto. Add salt and pepper to taste. Cover and let sit while you fry the cucumber cakes.

6 Combine all the ingredients for the cucumber cakes. If the mixture is too moist add a little flour. Heat the butter in a pan and fry 4 cakes.

Tip: Peel the asparagus from top to bottom, overlapping the strokes to make sure that no bits of peel are overlooked. White asparagus usually takes between ten and fifteen minutes to cook. Instead, boil them for only five minutes, then you can leave them in the pot, covered, for 20 minutes to half an hour to let them soften in the hot water. This will give you some leeway as far as time goes, and you don't have to worry so much about asparagus being overdone. In a pinch, you can always leave them in the water and heat them up before serving (but do not boil).

Chic serviettes

Anybody would agree that nice cloth serviettes look much more stylish than their paper cousins. You can make them yourself from sheets of nice fabric cut to about 50cm x 50 cm (20" x 20"). Look for absorbent fabric, linen or cotton are best. Or sew two different types of fabric together, then you can also use two different colours or two different materials – perhaps one matte and one shiny. Old serviettes can also be adapted to the style of the table, for example using textile paint to give them coloured edges.

Flickering candles

To prevent candle wax from being blown all over your nice tablecloths on a windy day, simply place the candlesticks on a table runner (or a nice piece of fabric). Attach a piece of plastic film (wrap) to the bottom of the runner with a double-sided piece of sticky tape, so that it will not be visible between the runner and the table cloth. The wax will not get through, try as it might.

Asparagus salad with truffle

500 g asparagus, boiled and cut into diagonal pieces – 1 egg, hardboiled, mashed fine – 50 g (fresh) truffle, one half cut into small pieces, the other thinly shaved (with a cheese slicer)
For the dressing: 2 tbsp white wine vinegar – 1 tbsp truffle oil – 1 tbsp maize-germ oil – 1 tbsp bouillon – 1 tsp red wine vinegar – salt

1 Combine all the ingredients for the dressing and salt to taste.
2 Mix in the egg and the truffle pieces (but not the shavings). Briefly heat the dressing but do not let it come to the boil.
3 Divide the asparagus over 4 plates and drizzle with the dressing. Make sure that the egg and the truffle are evenly distributed.
4 Sprinkle with the truffle shavings.

The good life

Stuffed chicken fillets with field mustard mash

4 chicken fillets, each 150 g (5.25 oz), flattened
8 sage leaves
1 ball fresh mozzarella, sliced
salt and pepper
butter or oil for frying

For the field mustard mash:
2 kg (4.4 lbs) potatoes, peeled and boiled
500 g (17.5 oz) field mustard, very finely chopped
2 dl (7 oz) milk
50 g (1.75 oz) butter

1 Preheat the oven to 150 °C (300° F or gas mark 2). Place 2 sage leaves on each chicken fillet and top this with the mozzarella.

2 Roll or fold up the fillets and stick a toothpick through them to keep them closed if necessary. Sprinkle with a little salt and pepper.

3 Heat the oil or butter and fry the fillets until brown. Place in the oven for 20 minutes to finish cooking.

4 While the chicken fillets cook, heat the milk for the mashed potatoes and melt the butter in the hot milk.

5 Mash the potatoes or press them through a potato ricer. Whisk in the milk and add salt and pepper to taste.

6 When the mashed potatoes are good and hot, remove from the heat and stir in the field mustard. Serve the chicken fillets on a mound of mashed potatoes.

Tip: Delicious with stir-fried spring vegetables: snow peas, sugar snap peas, green peas, broccoli florets, baby corn...

Pancetta-wrapped rack of lamb

2 racks of lamb
8 slices pancetta or smoked bacon
1 tbsp olive oil

For the antiboise sauce:
2 tomatoes, seeded and diced
½ bunch of basil, finely chopped
1 clove of garlic, very finely chopped
2 dl (7 oz) olive oil
balsamic vinegar.

1 Combine the tomato, basil, garlic and oil.
2 Preheat the oven to 100° C (220° F or gas mark ¼).
3 Slice the racks up two bones at a time. From each of these double ribs, remove one bone so that you are left with one large chop. Make 8 portions in this way.
4 Wrap each portion in pancetta and fry in the oil until nice and brown on each side. Place in the oven for 20 minutes to finish cooking.
5 Ladle the antiboise onto the plates. Drizzle with a little balsamic vinegar and sprinkle with sea salt. Top with the meat.

The done thing

Though many people might feel it's a bit corny, following proper etiquette does give you one big advantage: you always know what to do. Of course, you can set the table however you like – but if you want to try for something chic, go the official route: forks to the left of the plate, knives and the soup spoon to the right. The utensils which are to be used first are positioned on the outside, ranging inward in the order of courses. Dessert spoon above the plate. Bread plate above and to the left. Water glass in the middle above the plate. Wine glasses to the right above the knives: red wine on the left and white on the right. However you do it, the thing to remember is that a table which is set with care adds a lot to the overall ambience of a meal. The introduction to this book will give you some ideas about creating a certain atmosphere at your table.

Oysters & champagne

An ideal aperitif! Exceptionally chic, ready in no time and something even for people who have never had raw oysters before: they're guaranteed to want a nibble once they see them. Open the oysters (the liquid should stay inside) and check to make sure there are no hard pieces of shell mixed in. Keep covered in the refrigerator until ready to serve. Make a vinaigrette of equal parts olive oil and balsamic vinegar and throw some of this in, perhaps with a little very finely chopped shallot or chives, right before serving. Or serve the oysters with lemon wedges. The only other thing you have to worry about is getting the champagne ice-cold.

Sweet pepper roll-ups with parsley puree filling

2 sweet red peppers
2 potatoes, peeled and boiled
1 bunch parsley, finely chopped
1 tbsp butter
juice of 1 lemon

For the parsley oil:
1 bunch parsley, finely chopped
1 clove of garlic,
very finely chopped
5 tbsp olive oil
salt and pepper

1 Preheat the oven to 200° C (400° F or gas mark 6). Roast the peppers on a sheet of aluminium foil for 30 minutes. Remove from the oven, fold the foil around the peppers and set them aside to cool.

2 Remove the peel and seeds; this is easiest under cold running water. Cut the peppers in half lengthwise. Try to make nice even cuts.

3 Using a handheld blender or potato press, puree the potatoes with the parsley and butter. Season with salt and lemon juice to taste.

4 Spread the puree over the pepper halves and roll these up. Keep chilled until ready to serve.

5 For the parsley oil, combine parsley, garlic and oil, blending with a handheld blender until smooth. Add salt and pepper to taste.

6 Serve the roll-ups cold or heat them up in an oven at 150° C (300° F or gas mark 2) for 5 minutes. Slice into rounds if desired. Drizzle the parsley oil over top or serve on the side.

4 sheets puff pastry
1 tomato, sliced
1 red onion, cut into half-rings
4 tbsp capers
400 g (14 oz) Mascarpone
2 egg yolks
1 sprig of thyme,
very finely chopped
2 cloves of garlic,
very finely chopped
2 egg whites, beaten stiff
2 tbsp pine nuts, toasted
butter for greasing
small amount of flour or
bread crumbs
salt and pepper
4 pie dishes
For the sherry sauce:
1 tbsp olive oil
½ onion, very finely chopped
½ carrot, chopped
1 celery stalk,
chopped
1 dl (3.5 oz) dry white wine
1 dl (3.5 oz) sherry
2.5 dl (1 cup) vegetable stock
2 dl (7 oz) single cream

Mediterranean savoury pie with sherry sauce

1 Preheat the oven to 200 °C (400° F or gas mark 6). Grease the pie dishes with the butter and cover them with the puff pastry.
2 Using a fork, poke holes in the pastry and sprinkle with flour or bread crumbs; this will give you a firmer base.
3 Arrange the tomato, onion and capers in the pie dishes.
4 Combine the Mascarpone, egg yolks, thyme and garlic. Fold in the egg white. Season with salt and pepper to taste.
5 Fill the pie dishes with this mixture. Sprinkle with pine nuts.
6 Bake the pies at 200° C (400° F or gas mark 6) for 10 minutes, then turn the oven to 150° C (300° F or gas mark 2) and bake for 20 minutes.
7 While the pies cook, make the sherry sauce: Briefly sauté the vegetables in the oil. Pour in the wine, sherry, stock and single cream. Keep on very low heat for half an hour to let the flavours marry (or boil down briefly for a thicker sauce). Strain and season with salt and pepper to taste.

Turkey with truffle sauce

400 g (14 oz) turkey fillet – 200 g (7 oz) leek, cut into large pieces – 1 tbsp oil
For the dressing: 1 tbsp white wine vinegar – 1 tbsp truffle oil – 1 tbsp bouillon – 1 tsp honey – 1 tsp mustard – 1 egg yolk – 2 dl (7 oz) maize-germ oil

1 Combine all the ingredients for the dressing except the oil, mixing well. Stir in the oil in a thin slow stream, then salt to taste.
2 Sprinkle the turkey with a little salt and fry the fillets in a small amount of oil until brown and cooked through. Cut them into thin slices.
3 Stir-fry the leek in a little oil until just tender.
4 Arrange the leek over 4 plates and top with the turkey. Ladle the dressing over and around it.

A few home-made crisps can be quite attractive as a finishing touch to a dish, or as a tasty snack before the meal. For Serrano crisps: Lay pieces of Serrano ham (or Parma ham) on unwaxed baking paper and roast in a preheated oven at 180° C (350° F or gas mark 4) or until they are light brown and crunchy. Vegetable crisps: cut your choice of carrots, beetroot, parsnips, sweet potatoes, celery root, etc. into long, thin slices (this is easiest with the slicing blade of a food processor or on a mandolin). Fry the slices in batches in peanut oil at 180° C (350° F or gas mark 4) until golden brown and crunchy (2 to 3 minutes). If desired, sprinkle them with coarse sea salt and chilli powder. If serving the crisps as a snack, chutney is an excellent dip for the side.

Fancy crisps

Veal with avocado sauce

4 veal collops, approx. 120 g each
2 orange or lemon, peeled
1 ripe avocado, diced
1 shallot, very finely chopped
1 tbsp olive oil
3 dl (10.5 oz) bouillon
1 dl (3.5 oz) crème fraîche
50 g (1.75 oz) butter

1 Remove the peel and pith from the orange or lemon. Separate the segments, catching the juice.
2 Drizzle the juice over the pieces of avocado.
3 Sauté the shallot in the oil. Add the bouillon and bring to a boil.
4 Add the crème fraîche and avocado to the bouillon, stirring well. Heat through, then add the citrus segments.
5 Fry the veal collops in the butter for 5 minutes or until cooked through. Serve with the sauce.

Tip: do not boil the sauce, otherwise the avocado will turn bitter.

4 fillets of sole
500 g (17.5 oz) mussels,
boiled
12 king prawns
1 l (1qt) fish stock
½ tbsp olive oil
4 metal cooking rings,
greased

For the sauce:
½ bunch parsley,
finely chopped
½ bunch mint,
finely chopped
½ bunch basil,
finely chopped
1 clove of garlic,
very finely chopped
1 tbsp capers,
finely chopped
2 gherkins,
finely chopped
4 anchovies,
finely chopped
1 tsp mustard
1 tbsp red wine vinegar
4 tbsp olive oil

Seafood-stuffed fillet of sole

1 Preheat the oven to 150 °C (300° F or gas mark 2). Heat the fish stock until it comes to a boil, then turn off the heat.
2 Place the sole in the stock for 2 minutes, then carefully remove.
3 Wrap the sole around the inside of the cooking rings.
4 Shell half of the mussels. Sauté the prawns for 1 minute in the olive oil.
5 Combine all the ingredients for the sauce and season with salt and pepper to taste.
6 Fill the cooking rings with the prawns and mussels. Bake for 4 minutes in the preheated oven, then carefully remove from the rings and place on 4 plates.
7 Pour on the sauce and garnish with the remaining mussels.

Duck leg confit pie

6 duck legs
3 tbsp oil
1 l (1 qt) goose fat (ask at the poultry counter)
1 bay leaf
1 tsp sea salt
4 white asparagus stalks, peeled and diced
½ bunch parsley, finely chopped
1 sweet red pepper, diced
200 g (7 oz) haricots verts, cut into small pieces
salt and pepper

1 Preheat the oven to 125° C (250° F or gas mark 1/2). Sprinkle the duck legs with salt and pepper and fry in 1 tbsp oil until nice and brown.
2 Heat the goose fat, add the bay and salt and pour into a heat-resistant dish.
3 Place the duck legs in this and roast in the pre-heated oven for 5 hours.
4 When done, remove from the oven and allow to cool. When cool enough to handle, remove the meat from the bone.
5 Add the parsley and 1 tbsp of the asparagus pieces and mix well.
6 Shape the meat mixture into 4 tartlets using a biscuit (cookie) cutter, ramekin or other circular mould. Heat briefly in the oven.
7 Heat the remaining oil and stir-fry the diced veggies until they are just tender.
8 Place a tartlet in the middle of each plate and arrange the vegetables around it.

Tip: 'Confit de canard', or duck confit, can be kept for a long time due to its fat content – at least two to three months.

179

Flowers on the table

Flowers are always brilliant eye-catchers to top off a stylish table setting. Why not break the mould and go for a different look than the typical centre-piece bouquet? Clean some old marmalade jars, one for each guest, and fill each one with a low-trimmed Gerber daisy or other flower, or a mini-bouquet of daisies, buttercups and a spray of attractive grasses, tied with a bit of ribbon or string. It's also a nice touch to set single flowers on top of the folded serviette on each plate, or to stick one behind the serviette ring – throw in a sprig of aromatic herbs and your guests will be presented with quite a flourish. If you don't have serviette rings, a broad piece of ribbon will work too. Or even sprinkle flower petals across the table for a truly romantic effect.

flowers on the table

Tenderloin with herb mustard

1 x 500 g (17.5 oz) tenderloin
1 tbsp mustard
½ bunch parsley, finely chopped
½ bunch basil, finely chopped
1.5 dl (5.25 oz) balsamic vinegar
0.5 dl (1.75 oz) bouillon
1 tbsp honey
12 shallots
1 kg (2.2 lbs) potatoes
clump of butter
dash of milk
250 g (8.75 oz) oyster mushrooms
1 tbsp butter or oil

1 Preheat the oven to 180° C (350° F or gas mark 4). Combine the mustard and the herbs. Drag the meat through the herb mixture, making sure it's coated on all sides.
2 Put the tenderloin in a roasting dish and place in the oven for 10 minutes. Remove the meat and wrap in aluminium foil, then set in a warm place.
3 Combine the balsamic vinegar, bouillon and honey. Boil this mixture until it takes on a syrupy consistency.
4 Bring a pot of water to a boil and blanch the shallots for 15 minutes. Remove and stir into the vinegar sauce.
5 Puree the potatoes, milk and butter until smooth and fluffy.
6 Fry the oyster mushrooms in butter or oil until nice and brown, then stir into the potatoes. Season with salt and pepper to taste.
7 Place a mound of the potato mixture in the middle of each plate. Cut the tenderloin into thin slices and arrange on top of the potatoes. Ladle the sauce over and around it.

The menu

A whimsical touch for your table: create restaurant-style menus and place them in nice picture frames.

Sweet dreams

Slices of dried fruit make exquisite garnishes for desserts: drench very thin slices of apple, peach, mango, banana etc. in simple syrup and place on an ungreased tray to dry in a warm oven.

Tip: You don't need to feel limited to apples for this dessert; try other fruits of your choice. Soft fruits, such as raspberries, will turn into a sumptuous compote in the oven.

Apple crumble tarts

For 6 tarts

For the crumble (dough):
180 g (6.35 oz) flour
225 g (8.75 oz or 1 cup) sugar
100 g (3.5 oz) butter, cold, in small pieces

For the filling:
6 Gold-Rennet (or Jonagold or Golden Delicious) apples, cut into 2 cm (0.8") thick wedges
100 g (3.5 oz) sugar
2 tbsp lemon juice
1 tsp ground cinnamon
3 tbsp chopped walnuts

1. Combine the flour and sugar and add the cold pieces of butter.
2. Make the crumble dough by rubbing all the ingredients between your fingers.
3. Combine the apple wedges with 100 g (3.5 oz) sugar, the lemon juice, cinnamon and walnuts.
4. Arrange the wedges on the bottom of greased single-serving tart pans.
5. Crumble the dough over top and bake at 180° C (350° F or gas mark 4) for 40 minutes.
6. Serve at room temperature with whipped cream and/or ice cream.

Tip: You can make thin swirls of chocolate by melting bittersweet chocolate or couverture and squeezing it in a thin stream out of a paper cornet or pastry bag.

150 g (5.25 oz) bittersweet chocolate
5 egg yolks
6 tbsp sugar
2.5 dl (1 cup) cream
6 egg whites
1 tbsp Tia Maria or other coffee liqueur

Chocolate mousse

1 Melt the chocolate in a bain-marie, or double-boiler.
2 Beat the egg yolks with the sugar to form a stiff, foamy mixture. Add to the melted chocolate.
3 Whip the cream until almost stiff.
4 Beat the egg whites until stiff peaks form.
5 Add the Tia Maria or other liqueur to the chocolate. Fold in the cream and egg whites.
6 Fill 4 cups with the mousse and chill for 1 hour in the refrigerator.

Mascarpone brûlé

4 egg yolks
60 g (2 oz) sugar
350 g (12 oz) Mascarpone
1 dl (3.5 oz) cream
1 tsp orange zest (freshly grated rind)
50 g (1.75 oz) chocolate couverture, in pieces
2 tbsp brown sugar

1 Beat the egg yolks with the sugar.
2 Mix in the Mascarpone and cream together with
   1 tsp orange zest.
3 Divide the mixture over 4 greased ramekins or other
   small dishes. Put the ramekins in a heat-resistant
   dish filled with water and place in a pre-heated oven
   at 150° C (300° F or gas mark 2) for 45 minutes.
4 Remove from the oven and let the ramekins cool,
   then fold the couverture into the mascarpone
   mixture.
5 Allow to cool further.
6 Sprinkle the ramekins with brown sugar and toast the
   top with a brulee torch or under the broiler.

White wine sabayon with fresh summer fruit

200 g (7 oz) strawberries, cut into pieces – 200 g
(7 oz) blueberries – 200 g (7 oz) red currants – 200 g
(7 oz) raspberries – 200 g (7 oz) blackberries –
For the sabayon: – 4 egg yolks – 50 g (1.75 oz)
sugar – 2 dl (7 oz) dry white wine

1 Combine the egg yolks, sugar and wine. Beat
   this mixture in a bain-marie, or double-boiler,
   until thick and creamy.
2 Divide the fruit over 4 plates or small bowls and
   ladle the sabayon over top.

Tip: Garnish with chocolate curls. You can make these by melting 100 grams of couverture and pouring this into thin sheets on a flat surface. Cut the chocolate off right before it starts to harden. If necessary, you can store the curls in the freezer in an air-tight container.

Champagne soufflé with mango coulis

0.8 dl (2.8 oz) champagne
2 eggs, separated
15 g (0.5 oz) sugar
15 g (0.5 oz) flour
45 g (1.5 oz) full-fat yoghurt
1 ½ sheets of gelatin, soaked in cold water
50 g (1.75 oz) confectioner's sugar
2 mangos, very finely chopped
4 greased metal cooking rings

For the mango coulis:
1 mango, peeled and pitted
2.5 dl (1 cup) water
½ tsp sugar
dash of lemon juice

1 Combine the egg yolks, sugar and flour and stir until smooth.

2 Bring the champagne and yoghurt to a boil. Remove from the heat and stir into the egg yolk mixture. Strain the mixture through a sieve.

3 Drain the gelatin and stir it into the yoghurt mixture. Continue stirring until the gelatin dissolves. Allow the mixture to cool until it begins to thicken.

4 Beat the egg whites with the confectioner's sugar until stiff and fold into the champagne mixture.

5 Fill the cooking rings halfway and top each one with 1 heaping tablespoon mango. Fill with the remaining mixture. Chill the soufflés for approx. 6 hours or until stiff.

6 While the soufflés chill, make the mango coulis: boil the water, dissolve the sugar and take this simple syrup off the heat to cool.

7 In a food processor or with a handheld blender, puree the peeled mango together with the simple syrup. Add a few drops of lemon juice to taste.

8 Remove the soufflés from the cooking rings and place them on 4 plates. Pour on the mango coulis.

menus

Menu 1
Refined simplicity

spring salad with polenta croutons (p. 161)
wine: Chardonnay (not barrel-aged); try a South African or Australian, for example
***
garlic soup (p. 162)
***
stuffed chicken fillets on field mustard mash (p. 170)
wine: heavy, full-bodied white wine, a Spanish or Portuguese
***
apple crumble tarts (p. 182)
wine: German or Austrian Beerenauslese or Trockenbeerenauslese

Preparation
For the grocery shopping, see the ingredients lists accompanying the recipes (p. 161, 162, 170, 182). **One day before:** Make the croutons and keep them in an air-tight container. Make the soup.

The day of
Get the chicken fillets ready to go in the oven (do not fry them yet). Get the apple crumble tarts ready for baking. Peel the potatoes and cut the field mustard. **One hour before:** Bake the pies. Toss the salad at the very last minute. Wait until the soup is gone to finish making the main course.

3x faster
Delegate: Have someone else peel the potatoes and cut the field mustard. **Simplify:** Buy good-quality croutons from the deli or supermarket. **Leave out:** Leave out the soup if necessary...

Menu 2

The never-ending meal

smoked trout with ginger dressing (p. 160)
wine: Champagne brut or Cava.

***

asparagus soup with scallops (p. 165)

***

sweet pepper roll-ups with parsley puree filling (p. 173)
wine: Grüner Veltliner

***

veal with avocado sauce (p. 177)
wine: A barrel-aged chardonnay from North or South America

***

tenderloin with herb mustard, balsamic vinegar and shallots (p. 181)
wine: a full-bodied Merlot or Cabernet Sauvignon

***

white wine sabayon with fresh summer fruit (p. 184)
wine: Asti Spumante

Preparation

For the grocery shopping, see the ingredients lists accompanying the recipes (p. 160, 165, 173, 177, 181, 184). For each course, take a half-portion per person. Use small plates and coffee cups for the soup. **One day before:** Smoke the trout and make the dressing. Make the asparagus soup. Make the sweet pepper roll-ups and the parsley oil. And the balsamic sauce for the tenderloin.

The day of:

Make the avocado sauce. Peel the potatoes and prepare the tenderloin. Clean the fruit. **One hour before:** Get all the ingredients ready for each dish. At this point all the dishes require but a finishing touch. You can do this at the very last minute.

Menu 3
Decadent party menu

asparagus salad with truffles (p. 168)

***

seafood-stuffed fillet of sole (p. 178)
wine: dry white Bourgogne, such as a Chablis or Pouilly-Fumé

***

pancetta-wrapped rack of lamb (p. 171)
wine: red Bordeaux

***

champagne soufflé with mango coulis (p. 185)
wine: Champagne demi-sec

Preparation

Consider the oysters as an amuse-bouche. For the grocery shopping, see the ingredients lists accompanying the recipes (p. 168, 178, 171, 185). You will also need: mixed spring vegetables for the lamb. **One day before:** Make the dessert and the salsa verde for the sole. Prep the lamb and make the antiboise sauce. Blanch the spring vegetables for the lamb (this way they will only need a few minutes in the wok).

The day of:

Peel the asparagus and keep them in a very moist towel (no longer than 2 hours). Make the truffle dressing. **One hour before:** Cook the asparagus. You can make the sole at the very last minute because it would be a culinary sin to reheat the ingredients.

3x faster

Delegate: Have someone else peel the asparagus and shell the mussels. **Simplify:** You can ask the butcher to prepare the lamb for you (make sure you ask in advance). If you are cooking for a large number of guests, then you can save a lot of time by presenting the sole not as a roll-up but as a normal fillet with the filling on the side. **Leave out:** Of course you wouldn't want to...

Cheese plate

When the sun goes down, the nice mature cheeses appear on the table. Just delicious, such a smörgåsbord of different cheeses. There is something for everyone: a creamy soft cheese, a nice farmhouse Cheddar, a sharp and crumbly bleu. And the end of the meal is nowhere in sight!

Of course, you can always serve the cheese plate before the sweet dessert. This is how they do it in France, and the rest of Europe as well usually. In England it's often the reverse: first the sweet dessert and then the cheese. The order can be decided by which wine you want to drink. If you opt for a red wine, then serve the cheese first, followed by the dessert. If you plan on serving a nice glass of port with the cheese (a fantastic combination!) then reverse the order.

Italian cheese board

- Fontina d'Aosta: a semi-hard cheese with a brown rind. When young, it has a milky flavour, while the older cheeses display an earthy, fruity aroma.

- Gorgonzola: a semi-soft Italian blue cheese with a creamy texture and a sharp, savoury taste.

- Parmigiano-Reggiano: aka Parmesan cheese. Good Parmesan has a sublimely full and complex flavour with a salty undertone.

- Robiola: A soft, moist and snow white cheese with a sweet milky aroma and a rather salty flavour.

- Taleggio: A semi-soft cheese with a pinkish orange washed rind. A full and fruity flavour with a long creamy aftertaste.

Cheese family

When picking out cheeses to serve, it's a big help to remember the five 'cheese families'. These are, consecutively: the goat's and sheep's cheeses; the white mould cheeses (such as brie); hard and semi-hard cheeses (such as Gouda); blue cheeses (Roquefort) and finally the red-rind cheeses (Port Salut). Choose one cheese from each family, then you won't need to worry about having enough variety. It's also fun to pick out different cheeses from a single country, with an Italian or French cheese board, for instance. But... it can be very tempting to overdo it. As with many things, a good rule of thumb is: better to stick with one or two excellent varieties than six mediocre ones. You can always pick out two or three cheeses from the examples given here. Other things to consider: farmhouse cheeses are almost always more flavourful than the factory versions. Your selection should also depend on which cheeses are just 'ripe', or perfectly mature at the moment. Ask at the cheese counter; if anybody knows, they should.

Just a taste

Take the cheese out of the refrigerator at the beginning of the meal so that it has a chance to reach the right temperature by the time you serve it. This is when the flavour is optimal – if the cheese it too cold, you won't be able to taste it so well. Arrange the cheeses on a cheese board with a different knife for each variety, or cut off slices from each one and make up plates for each guest. If you serve four different cheeses, you can reckon on 25 grams (0.9 oz) per person per variety. Serve the cheese with biscuits and fruit, vegetables or nuts: grapes, walnuts, slices or pear or apple, and celery stalks. Start with the mildest cheese and work your way up to the sharpest; this will let you best experience the range of flavours. A true joy for the senses – what a great finale to your meal!

English cheese board

- **Caerphilly:** a semi-hard cheese with a subtle flavour and tart, salty undertones of fresh citrus.

- **Lancashire:** Crumbly cheese with a salty flavour which strengthens as it matures, along with a grassy aroma.

- **Mature Cheddar:** a golden yellow cheese with a smooth, firm texture and a pronounced nutty flavour.

- **Stilton:** a semi-soft blue cheese with a sharp, nutty aroma and a fruity flavour. Traditionally eaten with port.

- **Wensleydale:** hard cheese with a firm yet crumbly texture. The aroma is rich, sweet and milky with grassy undertones while the flavour has citrus notes.

(Ref. from: Judy Ridgway,
The Cheese Companion)

index

Food 4 Friends